"Winter is the time fo
for good food and warmth,
for the touch of a friendly
hand and for a talk beside the
fire, it is time for home."

EDITH SITWELL (POET)

INTRODUCTION

Going 'cold turkey' on carbohydrates for a ketogenic diet can be easier for some than others. For me, at the start at least, I was missing bread a lot. I was surprised how much I missed being able to grab a piece of toast, a slice of pizza or a bagel! I also really missed potatoes, especially in the form of chips or French fries! It was also initially quite tough to cut out all the other comfort food that I craved when I was tired or stressed. No more cakes, cookies or pies – even for special occasions! I must confess that I may have broken those rules once or twice in the early days of going keto... However, with a little bit of effort and work, I managed to recreate some of my favorite carb-heavy dishes in a keto-friendly way. I discovered that there were some great substitutes for all that comfort food that I was craving! I also found it a great way to get the family involved at dinnertime. Dinner was no longer the stereotypical 'slab of meat with a salad or side of vegetables' and it was great to have the occasional dessert or treat again - guilt-free!

The recipes **do not** include highly processed or expensive low-carb ingredients. For example, rather than using 'low-carb pasta' from the superstore, spaghetti squash and zoodles are great low-carb, wholesome alternatives. I have tried to take this approach with all of the recipes.

All of the recipes have been designed with you in mind...

- **Provides you with more time to enjoy your life** – All of the recipes are quick to make (no gourmet meals with three hours of preparation).

- **Look forward to your meals** – These are some of the best recipes I know; they are delicious and full of flavor.

- **No cooking experience required** – They can be made by anyone.

- **Hassle-free shopping** – All of the ingredients can be easily found in your local store.

- **Mouthwatering** – All of the recipes come with full images.

This book is split into 10 sections according to the carbohydrate and meal type. Main dishes are separated by the carbohydrate type, from easy-bake bread to delicious traditional pastas. The remaining sections have some great suggestions for breakfast, snacks and desserts.

Thank you for purchasing this book. I hope you will give me the privilege of helping you create your own sustainable lifestyle on the ketogenic diet.

Elizabeth

TABLE OF CONTENTS

KETO SWEET EATS BONUS

BONUS KETO SWEET EATS

I am delighted you have chosen my book to help you start or continue on your keto journey. Temptation by sweet treats can knock you off course so, to help you stay on the keto track, I am pleased to offer you three mini ebooks from my 'Keto Sweet Eats Series', completely free of charge! These three mini ebooks cover how to make everything from keto chocolate cake to keto ice cream to keto fat bombs so you don't have to feel like you are missing out, whatever the occasion. Simply visit the link below to get your free copy of all three mini ebooks:

HTTP://KETOJANE.COM/CARBS

WHAT'S INSIDE?

The recipes in this book have been divided into ten different categories, according to the carbohydrate that has been substituted. Some categories are easier to prepare than others. Some categories are for days when you would like to spend a bit more time in the kitchen (like quiches and savory pies). Others allow you to prepare a delightful dish without much effort and with very little time. However, all recipes in this book have been created to be incredible, regardless of the time spent cooking!

Here is an overview of the recipe types and a few tips on how to get the best out of them:

- **Bread:** Regular bread does not fit into the keto diet, but that doesn't mean you should go without. There are some amazing low carb options included, and none require a bread maker. You can enjoy those sandwiches again!

- **Soups:** Soups are one of my go to comfort foods especially during the cooler months. They are easy to make, packed full of flavor, and add a nice boost of nutritional value. I have included some mouthwatering keto-friendly soups that are hearty, creamy, and so flavorful you won't even miss the carbohydrates.

- **Sauces:** I used to love adding salad dressings to my salads or tomato sauce to my pasta dishes but these just don't fit in my ketogenic lifestyle anymore. However, that doesn't mean that I don't miss enjoying them which is why I have created some easy keto-friendly sauces to go with some low-carb "pasta" dishes. The creamy alfredo sauce is to die for!

- **Slow Cooker Meats:** Nothing screams comfort food as much as a slow cooked meal. I love making keto-friendly comfort foods in a slow cooker because it brings out all of the flavors from each ingredient plus it takes very little prep, cook, and clean up time. Slow cooker meals guarantees that you will have a warm meal to come home to after a long day of work!

- **Potato:** There were days when I would crave potato salad... Maybe you feel the same. If so, you will find a solution to your potato cravings in this section. I have included some sweet potato recipes, which may concern some people. However, they are still low in carbs so you just need to ensure they fit in with your macros for the day. I am sure you will find the sweet potato nachos worth it!

- **Rice:** These are among the easiest and quickest recipes in the book. I would recommend using these as a quick and easy weekday meal. There are some great alternatives here, including my favorite, Apple Vanilla 'Rice' Pudding.

- **Pizza:** Pizza is such a versatile dish! Once you have mastered the low carb base, you can create your own keto pizza anytime. I have included recipes for some of my favorite pizzas to get you started.

- **Quiches and Savory Pies:** These recipes require more time to prepare. They are easy but need some patience to achieve the best results. Use them for special occasions and when you have an hour or so to spare.

- **Noodles/Pasta:** Melted cheese, sauces, Italian-inspired herbs... Here you can find them all! From traditional lasagna and spaghetti to some modern alternatives such as Cheesy Stuffed Zucchini.

- **Breakfasts**: It is important to get your day off to a good start! This section presents ideas for starting your day with great food -quick and easy recipes for weekdays and more indulgent recipes for brunch at the weekends.

- **Snacks:** Sometimes, three square meals a day is either not enough or not achievable – this is where snacks come in! Maybe you need an appetizer to welcome your dinner guests. You will find recipes for both occasions in this section.

- **Pies**: Enjoy delicious, sweet pies, from chocolate to coconut. A variety of pies for different occasions! The recipes in this section require a bit more time than the desserts, but they are worth the effort!

- **Desserts:** Life has to be sweet, even on a keto diet! Here you will find everything from mug cakes to quickly satisfy your cravings, hazelnut brownies to eat after dinner and Snickerdoodles for a little treat to enjoy with a cup of coffee!

HOW THIS BOOK WORKS

This cookbook contains helpful cooking tips to help you get the best results possible. There are also serving suggestions included to give you an idea about what each of these dishes pairs well with.

You will also notice there are five symbols on the top right hand side of each recipe. A key to these symbols is set out below:

PREPARATION TIME:

Time required to prepare the recipe. This does not include cooking time.

COOKING TIME:

Time required to cook the recipe. This does not include the preparation time.

SERVINGS:

How many servings each recipe requires. This can be adjusted; for example, by doubling the quantity of all of the ingredients, you can make twice as many servings.

DIFFICULTY LEVEL:

1: An easy to make recipe that can be put together with just a handful of ingredients and in a short amount of time.

2: These recipes are a little more difficult and time consuming, but are still easy enough even for beginners!

3: A more advanced recipe for the adventurous cook! You will not see too many level 3 recipes in this book. These recipes are great for when you have a little bit more time to spend in the kitchen, and when you want to make something out of the ordinary.

Cost:

$:   A low budget everyday recipe.

$$:   A middle of the road, moderately priced recipe. The majority of the recipes you will find in this book are considered a level $$ on the cost scale.

$$$:   A more expensive recipe that is great for serving at a family gathering or party. These recipes tend to contain pricy ingredients such as higher quality meat products. You will not see too many level $$$ recipes in this book, but there are a few that you can make to impress your guests with!

DIETARY LABELS

Within this book, you will notice that there are dietary labels. These will indicate whether a recipe is gluten free, dairy free or vegetarian. Please note that many recipes can be made dairy free by removing the added cheese, or by substituting the milk or cream for coconut milk. Each recipe will also be labeled if it is gluten free. Although the majority of the recipes are gluten free, due to the variations in certain product ingredients, not all recipes will be marked gluten free. If you wish to make all recipes gluten free, be sure to check the food label on the ingredients you buy. You will also notice that if a recipe is not labeled as Paleo-friendly that I have made some suggestions on how to make most of the recipes Paleo-friendly by swapping out certain ingredients.

GF: Gluten free

DF: Dairy free

V: Vegetarian

P: Paleo

RECIPE NOTES

TAILOR THE RECIPES TO FIT YOUR PREFERENCES...

These recipes have been created with the following aims:

1. Simple to make

2. Delicious

3. Easily sourceable ingredients

However, there is not a one-size-fits-all recipe, everyone has different tastes and some have allergies. Consider the recipes a guideline that you can then customize to your own taste or adapt slightly to use what you have in the cupboards.

- Not a fan of thyme? Consider switching it with oregano - or leave it out entirely.

- No red pepper in your cupboards? Just use some normal black pepper instead.

- Not keen on Gouda cheese? Try mozzarella instead.

- Prefer your eggs a bit runnier? Cook them for slightly less time.

- Will four servings be too much? Simply halve the ingredients to create two servings.

- No spiralizer? Just cut into strips or use a vegetable peeler.

- Want more sweetness? Adjust the amount of sugar substitute according to your taste.

I have included some suggestions throughout for alternatives, but I could not list every single one. Only you know what your preferences are, so have some fun with it and play around with different ingredients and recipes.

Also, consider mixing up the recipes as they have been designed to be flexible. Mix some of the main dishes with a side dish and, of course, treat yourself with one of the delicious desserts!

For avoidance of doubt, the measurements in each recipe should be interpreted as follows:

TBSP. = tablespoon

TSP. = teaspoon

CUP = a US Cup

Once again, thank you for purchasing this book. I really appreciate you allowing me to help you with your diet and health in this way.

I would also appreciate any feedback you have. If you could leave an honest review, it would really help others to benefit from this book since few people buy books from Amazon without checking out the reviews first.

It will only take two minutes and the link below will take you straight there:

http://ketojane.com/carbreview

If you have any queries, please email me at: **elizabeth@ketojane.com**

Elizabeth

YOU MAY ALSO LIKE

Please visit the below link for other books by the author

http://ketojane.com/books

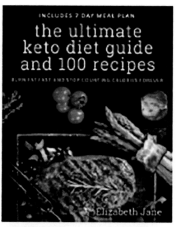

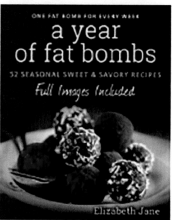

BREAD

TRADITIONAL SANDWICH BREAD

GF DF

Difficulty level : 2

Cost : $$

15 mins

45 mins

Serves 8

INGREDIENTS:

- ½ cup sifted coconut flour
- ¼ cup sifted gluten-free flour
- 6 room temperature eggs, separated
- ½ cup coconut oil
- 1 ½ teaspoons baking powder
- ¼ teaspoon salt
- 3 tablespoons water
- 1 tablespoon apple cider vinegar

DIRECTIONS:

1. Preheat your oven to 350°F, grease an 8 ½ by 4 ½ loaf pan with oil, and place a piece of parchment paper on the bottom of the pan.

2. Start by creaming the coconut oil in a food processor. Add in the egg yolks one at a time, placing the egg whites into a separate mixing bowl. Pulse to combine the coconut oil and egg yolks.

3. Add in the sifted coconut and gluten-free flour, baking powder, apple cider vinegar, water and salt, and pulse one more time until combined.

4. In the mixing bowl, beat the egg whites with a handheld mixer until stiff peaks form.

5. Fold the coconut flour mixture into the egg whites, and mix just until combined.

6. Pour into the prepped loaf pan and bake for 40-45 minutes, covering with aluminum foil halfway through to prevent the top of the loaf from burning.

7. Allow the bread to cool in the pan for 15 minutes before slicing.

8. Cover and store in the fridge for 3–4 days.

. . . .

Serving suggestion: Use this bread as you would traditional sandwich bread. This bread is kid-approved and pairs great with peanut butter and jelly!

Baking tips: If you want to turn this into a cinnamon raisin bread, add 1 teaspoon of cinnamon and 2 tablespoons of raisins to the mix.

NUTRITION FACTS (PER SERVING)

• Total Carbohydrates: 8g	% calories from:
• Dietary Fiber: 4g	• Fat: 80%
• Protein: 6g	• Carbohydrates: 8%
• Total Fat: 18g	• Protein: 12%
• Net Carbs: 4g	
• Calories: 209	

5 MINUTE NAAN BREAD

(GF) (DF) (P)

 Difficulty level : 1

 Cost : $

 5 mins

 5 mins

 Serves 4

INGREDIENTS:

- 1 cup almond flour
- 1 cup full fat coconut milk
- 1 pinch sea salt
- ¼ tsp. black pepper
- 1 tsp. onion powder
- 1 tsp. garlic powder
- 1 Tbsp. coconut oil

DIRECTIONS:

1. Mix all of the ingredients together and heat the coconut oil in a large pan over medium heat.

2. Pour a quarter of the batter into the pan and cook on one side until the naan begins to puff up - this may take a couple of minutes. Flip the naan over and cook the other side for 2-3 minutes. Repeat this to make four naan breads.

3. Serve warm.

Serving suggestions: Serve with butter or ghee and a dash of garlic powder.

Cut the bread into triangular pieces and dip in hummus.

Cooking tip: Wait until one side is well cooked before flipping to avoid the bread falling apart.

NUTRITION FACTS (PER SERVING)

- Total Carbohydrates: 10g
- Dietary Fiber: 5
- Protein: 8g
- Total Fat: 32g
- Net Carbs: 5g
- Calories: 332

% calories from:
- Fat: 87%
- Carbohydrates: 12%
- Protein: 10%

GARLIC ROLLS GF

 Difficulty level : 1

 Cost : $$

 10 mins

 20 mins

 Serves 18

INGREDIENTS:

- 1 cup almond flour
- 1 cup dry Parmesan cheese, grated
- 1 egg, beaten
- 1 Tbsp. & 1 tsp. garlic powder
- ½ tsp. salt
- 2 Tbsp. butter, melted
- ¼ cup olive oil

DIRECTIONS:

1. Preheat the oven to 350°F and line a baking sheet with parchment paper.

2. Whisk the olive oil and 1 teaspoon of garlic powder together in a bowl and set aside.

3. In a separate bowl, whisk together the almond flour, Parmesan cheese, salt and 1 tablespoon of garlic powder.

4. Add in the egg and melted butter, and stir.

5. Form into 18 rolls and place onto the parchment lined baking sheet.

6. Bake for about 18 minutes, turning halfway through.

7. After the garlic rolls are done baking, brush with the olive oil and garlic mix.

8. Enjoy while warm!

Cooking Tips: If you would like a more Italian flavored garlic roll, add in 1 teaspoon of Italian seasoning and half a teaspoon of oregano.

Adjust the size of the rolls according the number of portions you require, but adjust the baking time accordingly – larger rolls require more baking time.

Serving Suggestions: Serve with marinara or pesto sauce for a traditional Italian flavor.

NUTRITION FACTS (PER SERVING)

- Total Carbohydrates: 2g
- Dietary Fiber: 1g
- Protein: 3g
- Total Fat: 9g
- Net Carbs: 1g
- Calories: 98

- % calories from:
- Fat: 83%
- Carbohydrates: 8%
- Protein: 12%

CRANBERRY
PUMPKIN SEED BREAD (GF) (DF)

Difficulty level : 2

Cost : $$

10 mins

40 mins

Serves 8

INGREDIENTS:

- 6 eggs, beaten
- ½ cup coconut oil, melted
- 1 tsp. pure vanilla extract
- ¼ cup erythritol (use raw honey for a Paleo version)
- ½ cup coconut flour, sifted
- ½ tsp. salt
- ¼ tsp. gluten free baking powder (use baking soda for a Paleo version)
- 1 Tbsp. pumpkin pie spice (be sure this is a spice blend free from any added ingredients or fillers)
- 1 tsp. cinnamon
- ½ cup fresh cranberries, pitted
- ¼ cup pumpkin seeds

DIRECTIONS:

1. Preheat the oven to 350°F and grease a loaf pan with coconut oil. For best results, line the loaf pan with parchment paper to prevent the bread from sticking.

2. Cream the coconut oil and erythritol together. Stir in the egg yolks to the mixture, placing the egg whites in a separate bowl. Add in the remaining ingredients, minus the pumpkin seeds and cranberries, and mix again. Gently fold in the cranberries and pumpkin seeds last.

3. Whisk the egg whites with a handheld or standing mixer until hard peaks form, and fold the butter mixture into the eggs. Mix just until combined. Pour into the baking pan.

4. Bake for 35-40 minutes, or until the middle of the loaf is set.

5. Allow the bread to cool for 15 minutes before serving. To serve leftover bread, simply microwave or reheat in the oven and serve with a slab of butter.

Cooking Tips: If you want to bring out the pumpkin and cinnamon flavors, add in a pinch of nutmeg.

Stevia can be used in place of erythritol but you will only need about 1 teaspoon of liquid stevia as stevia is much sweeter.

If you wish to make these into muffins, pour the batter into a greased muffin tin and bake for 18-20 minutes.

NUTRITION FACTS (PER SERVING)

• Total Carbohydrates: 12g	% calories from:
• Dietary Fiber: 3g	• Fat: 80%
• Protein: 7g	• Carbohydrates: 21%
• Total Fat: 20g	• Protein: 12%
• Net Carbs: 9g	
• Calories: 226	

OLIVE MUFFINS

GF

 Difficulty level : 2

 Cost : $

 20 mins

 30 mins

Serves 6

INGREDIENTS:

- 2 ½ cups almond flour
- 1 cup heavy cream (use full-fat unsweetened coconut milk for a Paleo version)
- ¾ cup whole milk (use full-fat unsweetened coconut milk for a Paleo version)
- 4 eggs
- ½ cup black olives, pitted & halved
- ¼ cup butter, melted (use coconut oil for a Paleo version)
- 1 ½ tsp. gluten free baking powder (use baking soda for a Paleo version)
- ½ tsp. baking soda
- 1 tsp. freshly grated orange zest
- ½ tsp. salt

DIRECTIONS:

1. Preheat the oven to 350°F. Prepare a 6 cup muffin pan with non-stick cooking spray.

2. In a large bowl, whisk together the almond flour, baking soda, baking powder, freshly grated orange zest and salt.

3. In a separate bowl, whisk together the eggs, heavy cream, butter and milk.

4. Mix the wet ingredients into the dry and stir well to combine. Then, add the olives.

5. Divide the mixture evenly between the muffin cups and bake for about 30 minutes, until a toothpick inserted comes out clean.

. . . .

Cooking Tips: You can turn the muffins into a loaf of bread that can be sliced by using a greased loaf pan instead of a muffin pan.

Add some chopped ham and grated cheese to the mix, but consider reducing the salt in the recipe to balance the flavors.

NUTRITION FACTS (PER SERVING)

• Total Carbohydrates: 14g	% calories from:
• Dietary Fiber: 5g	• Fat: 84%
• Protein: 16g	• Carbohydrates: 10%
• Total Fat: 51g	• Protein: 18%
• Net Carbs: 9g	
• Calories: 544	

CHEDDAR BISCUITS GF

 Difficulty level : 1

 Cost : $

 10 mins

 12-15 mins

 Serves 8

INGREDIENTS:

- ⅓ cup coconut flour, sifted
- 3 eggs
- 4 Tbsp. coconut oil, melted
- ½ cup cheddar cheese, shredded
- 1 tsp. garlic powder
- ½ tsp. baking powder
- ½ tsp. salt

DIRECTIONS:

1. Start by preheating the oven to 350°F and lining a baking sheet with parchment paper.

2. Add the eggs to a mixing bowl and whisk.

3. Add in the remaining ingredients and whisk well.

4. Form into tablespoon-sized rounds and place onto the lined baking sheet.

5. Bake for 12-15 minutes or until lightly crispy on top.

NUTRITION FACTS (PER SERVING)

- Total Carbohydrates: 7g
- Dietary Fiber: 5g
- Protein: 6g
- Total Fat: 13g
- Net Carbs: 2g
- Calories: 165

% calories from:
- Fat: 73%
- Carbohydrates: 12%
- Protein: 15%

GUILT-FREE
CORN BREAD GF

 Difficulty level : 1

 Cost : $

 10 mins

 15-20 mins

 Serves 6

INGREDIENTS:

- 1 cup almond flour
- 2 eggs
- 3 Tbsp. coconut cream
- 2 Tbsp. heavy cream
- ¼ cup butter, melted
- 1 tsp. baking powder
- Coconut oil for greasing

DIRECTIONS:

1. Start by preheating the oven to 350°F and greasing a muffin tin with coconut oil.

2. Add all of the ingredients to a food processor and blend until smooth.

3. Pour the batter into the greased muffin tins and bake for 15-20 minutes or until a toothpick inserted into the center comes out clean.

4. Allow to cool for 5 minutes before removing from the muffin tins.

NUTRITION FACTS (PER SERVING)

- Total Carbohydrates: 2g
- Dietary Fiber: 1g
- Protein: 3g
- Total Fat: 15g
- Net Carbs: 1g
- Calories: 151

% calories from:
- Fat: 89%
- Carbohydrates: 3%
- Protein: 8%

ROSEMARY & THYME CRACKERS GF

 Difficulty level : 2

 Cost : $

 15 mins

 10 mins

 Serves 8

INGREDIENTS:

- 1 cup almond flour
- 1 cup cream cheese
- 1 egg
- 1 tsp. dried rosemary
- ½ tsp. dried thyme
- Pinch of salt & pepper

DIRECTIONS:

1. Start by preheating the oven to 400°F and lining a baking sheet with parchment paper.

2. Add all the ingredients to a food processor.

3. Add the dough to the baking sheet and use a rolling pin or a silicone spatula to spread the dough into a thin layer.

4. Cut the dough into small squares and bake for 5 minutes on each side.

5. Allow the crackers to cool and enjoy!

Cooking Tip: If you want a crispier cracker, cook for 6-7 minutes on each side.

NUTRITION FACTS (PER SERVING)

- Total Carbohydrates: 2g
- Dietary Fiber: 1g
- Protein: 4g
- Total Fat: 12g
- Net Carbs: 1g
- Calories: 130

% calories from:
- Fat: 84%
- Carbohydrates: 3%
- Protein: 13%

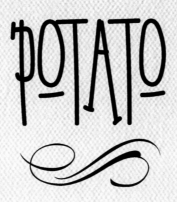

POTATO

GARLIC & CHIVE CAULIFLOWER MASH

GF

 Difficulty level : 1

 Cost : $

 10 mins

 20 mins

 Serves 3

INGREDIENTS:

- ½ tsp. garlic powder
- 1 head cauliflower, cut into florets
- 1 Tbsp. butter, at room temperature (use coconut oil for a Paleo version)
- 3 Tbsp. sour cream (eliminate for a Paleo version)
- ½ cup mozzarella cheese, grated (eliminate for a Paleo version)
- 2 Tbsp. chives, chopped
- 1 Tbsp. fresh oregano leaves, chopped
- Salt and pepper to taste

DIRECTIONS:

1. Place a steamer basket in a large pot and fill with about 2-3 inches of water.

2. Bring water to a boil and add the cauliflower. Steam for about 10 minutes, until tender.

3. Transfer the cauliflower to a food processor and blend on high speed for about 1 minute.

4. Add the butter, sour cream, garlic powder, oregano and mozzarella cheese. Season with salt and pepper and then process until smooth and creamy.

5. Garnish with chives and/or a pat of butter, if desired, and serve immediately.

Cooking Tip: Consider baking the cauliflower instead of steaming it. It requires additional time but it enhances the flavors.

NUTRITION FACTS (PER SERVING)

- Total Carbohydrates: 6g
- Dietary Fiber: 2g
- Protein: 8g
- Total Fat: 10g
- Net Carbs: 4g
- Calories: 140

% calories from:
- Fat: 64%
- Carbohydrates: 17%
- Protein: 23%

ONION & HERB CAULIFLOWER SALAD

GF

 Difficulty level : 1

 Cost : $

 10 mins

 15 mins

 Serves 3

INGREDIENTS:

- 1 head (about 2 cups) cauliflower, cut into small florets
- 3 hard-boiled eggs, chopped
- 5 Tbsp. sour cream (eliminate for a Paleo version)
- 4 Tbsp. heavy cream (eliminate for a Paleo version)
- ½ red bell pepper, seeded and chopped
- 2 Tbsp. red onion, minced
- 2 Tbsp. fresh oregano, chopped
- 2 Tbsp. fresh chives, chopped
- Salt and pepper to taste

DIRECTIONS:

1. Bring a large pot of water to a boil and cook the cauliflower for about 5 minutes, until tender. Drain and run under cold water.

2. In a large bowl, whisk together the sour cream and heavy cream until well combined.

3. Add the cauliflower, hard-boiled eggs, red onion, bell pepper, fresh oregano and chives. Season with salt and pepper and toss well to combine.

4. Refrigerate for at least 30 minutes before serving.

NUTRITION FACTS (PER SERVING)

- Total Carbohydrates: 10g
- Dietary Fiber: 4g
- Net Carbs: 6g
- Protein: 9g
- Total Fat: 16g
- Calories: 215

% calories from:
- Fat: 67%
- Carbohydrates: 19%
- Protein: 18%

TUMERIC SWEET POTATO
FRITERS GF

 Difficulty level : 1

 Cost : $

 15 mins

 15 mins

 Serves 4

INGREDIENTS:

- 1 small sweet potato, peeled
- ¼ cup almonds, finely chopped or grated
- ¼ cup flaxseed meal
- 1 egg
- ½ tsp. garlic powder
- ¼ tsp. ground cumin
- ¼ tsp. ground turmeric
- 2 Tbsp. butter (use coconut oil for a Paleo version)
- ¼ tsp. salt
- Freshly ground pepper to taste

DIRECTIONS:

1. Shred the sweet potato using your food processor or a box grater.

2. In a large bowl, whisk together the egg, turmeric powder, salt and 1 tablespoon of the butter.

3. Mix in the shredded sweet potatoes, almonds and flaxseed meal. Season with pepper.

4. In a large frying pan over medium heat, melt the remaining butter.

5. Once the butter is hot, drop the sweet potato mixture into the frying pan using a large spoon.

6. Cook for about 5 minutes, until golden brown. Flip and continue cooking for about 3 minutes, until the sweet potatoes are tender and the outside of the fritter is crisp and browned.

7. Serve immediately.

Serving Suggestions: Top with sour cream and herbs or serve with a dip. If your macros allow, try the traditional German choice of apple sauce or my favorite, Greek yogurt.

NUTRITION FACTS (PER SERVING)

- Total Carbohydrates: 11g
- Dietary Fiber: 5g
- Protein: 6g
- Total Fat: 15g
- Net Carbs: 6g
- Calories: 196

- % calories from:
- Fat: 69%
- Carbohydrates: 22%
- Protein: 12%

CREAMY MOCK POTATO SOUP

GF

 Difficulty level : 1

 Cost : $

 15 mins

 20 mins

 Serves 3

INGREDIENTS:

- 1 head cauliflower, chopped
- 4 Tbsp. fresh thyme, chopped
- ½ red onion, minced
- 1 garlic clove, minced
- 4 Tbsp. butter (use coconut oil for a Paleo version)
- 1 cup heavy cream (use full-fat unsweetened coconut milk for a Paleo version)
- 1 cup reduced sodium chicken or vegetable broth
- 1 cup mozzarella cheese, grated (eliminate for a Paleo version)
- ¼ tsp. ground cumin
- Salt and pepper to taste

DIRECTIONS:

1. Heat the butter in a saucepan over medium heat.
2. Add the onion and garlic, and sauté for about 3 minutes.
3. Add the cauliflower to the saucepan and season with salt, pepper and cumin.
4. Add the broth to the saucepan and increase the heat to medium-high. Bring to a simmer and cook for 7 minutes or until the cauliflower is tender and then turn off the heat.
5. Blend the soup in a food processor or using an immersion blender until it becomes smooth.
6. Return the soup to the saucepan. Add in heavy cream, fresh thyme and cheese. Cook for about 5 minutes over low heat.
7. Top with fresh thyme sprigs and serve.

Cooking Tips: Try adding beef or chicken cubes to this soup. Just brown the meat in a frying pan and add it to the saucepan along with the heavy cream, fresh thyme and cheese.

NUTRITION FACTS (PER SERVING)

- Total Carbohydrates: 12g
- Dietary Fiber: 4g
- Net Carbs: 8g
- Protein: 28g
- Total Fat: 39g
- Calories: 490

Percent Calories from:
- Carbs: 8%
- Protein: 23%
- Fat: 72%

ZESTY SWEET POTATO NACHOS

Difficulty level : 2

Cost : $$

15 mins

20 mins

Serves 5

GF

INGREDIENTS:

- 1 large sweet potato, thinly sliced
- 4 Tbsp. olive oil
- 1lb ground beef
- ¼ tsp. chili powder
- ¼ tsp. ground cumin
- ¼ tsp. paprika
- ½ bunch fresh parsley, roughly chopped
- 1 cup fresh mozzarella cheese, grated (eliminate for a Paleo version)
- Salt and pepper to taste

Guacamole

- 2 ripe avocados, peeled
- 4 Tbsp. lemon juice
- ½ red onion, minced
- ½ yellow bell pepper, chopped
- Salt and pepper to taste

DIRECTIONS:

1. Preheat the oven to 400°F.

2. Toss the sweet potato slices with the olive oil and transfer to a baking sheet. Spread evenly onto the baking sheet and season with salt and pepper. Bake for about 15 minutes, until crisp and golden brown.

3. While the sweet potatoes bake, heat a large frying pan over medium heat. Add the ground beef and season with paprika, chili powder, cumin, salt and pepper.

4. Cook until browned. Remove from the heat.

5. To prepare the guacamole: In a medium bowl, mash the avocados with a fork. Add the onion, bell pepper and lemon juice, and season with salt and pepper. Mix until well combined.

6. Transfer the baked sweet potatoes to a large platter. Top with the cheese, ground beef, guacamole and chopped parsley. Serve and enjoy!

. . . .

Cooking Tips: Try swapping the ground beef for shredded brisket or chicken.

Add chopped tomatoes and/or red bell pepper to the guacamole, as desired.

NUTRITION FACTS (PER SERVING)	
• Total Carbohydrates: 16g	% calories from:
• Dietary Fiber:8g	
• Protein: 38g	• Fat: 62%
• Total Fat: 37g	• Carbohydrates: 12%
• Net Carbs: 8g	• Protein: 28%
• Calories: 540	

RICE

VEGGIE FRIED RICE GF

 Difficulty level : 1

 Cost : $

 15 mins

 20 mins

 Serves 2

INGREDIENTS:

- ½ head cauliflower
- 5 Tbsp. frozen peas (eliminate for a Paleo version)
- ½ red onion, chopped
- 1 carrot, peeled and chopped
- 4 Tbsp. fresh thyme, chopped
- ¼ bunch fresh parsley, chopped
- 1 egg, lightly beaten
- 3 Tbsp. olive oil
- Salt and pepper to taste

DIRECTIONS:

1. In a food processor fitted with the shredding disc, shred the cauliflower. It should resemble rice once done. Alternatively, you can grate the cauliflower using a cheese grater.

2. Heat the olive oil in a large frying pan or wok. Add the onion, carrot and peas. Sauté until tender.

3. Push the vegetables to the side of the pan and add the egg. Scramble the egg using a spatula. When cooked, mix together with the vegetables.

4. Add the cauliflower "rice" to the egg and vegetable mixture and mix well.

5. Cook until the cauliflower is tender, for about 5 minutes. Then stir in the chopped parsley and thyme. Season with salt and pepper to taste.

Cooking Tips: Give it a kick by adding some chili powder or hot sauce.

Serving Suggestions: Serve as a quick and delicious meal or as a side dish.

NUTRITION FACTS (PER SERVING)

- Total Carbohydrates: 15g
- Dietary Fiber: 6g
- Protein: 7g
- Total Fat: 23g
- Net Carbs: 9g
- Calories: 280

% calories from:
- Fat: 74%
- Carbohydrates: 21%
- Protein: 10%

BASIL (GF) PARSNIP RICE

 Difficulty level : 1

 Cost : $

 10 mins

 20 mins

 Serves 3

INGREDIENTS:

- 1 parsnip, peeled
- 3 cups cauliflower florets
- ¼ cup fresh basil, chopped
- ½ onion, minced
- 3 Tbsp. butter (use coconut oil for a Paleo version)
- Salt and pepper to taste

DIRECTIONS:

1. In a food processor fitted with the shredding disc, shred the parsnip and cauliflower. Alternatively, you can use a cheese grater.

2. Heat the butter in a large frying pan over medium heat. Add the shredded parsnip and cauliflower, as well as the minced onion. Sauté for about 5 minutes until they begin to soften.

3. Reduce the heat to low, stir in the fresh basil, cover and allow to cook for about 8 minutes. Season with salt and pepper to taste.

4. Serve alongside a fish or chicken dish.

Cooking Tip: Using the food processor to shred the vegetables allows you to choose the desired texture of the rice.

NUTRITION FACTS (PER SERVING)

- Total Carbohydrates: 13g
- Dietary Fiber: 5g
- Protein: 3g
- Total Fat: 12g
- Net Carbs: 9g
- Calories: 160

% calories from:
- Fat: 68%
- Carbohydrates: 33%
- Protein: 8%

CREAMY CHICKEN AND "RICE" SOUP

Difficulty level : 2

Cost : $

15 mins

25 mins

Serves 3

GF

INGREDIENTS:

- 2 cups cooked chicken, shredded
- 1 head cauliflower
- ½ red onion, minced
- 4 cups fresh mushrooms, chopped
- 1 carrot, peeled and chopped
- 2 cloves garlic, minced
- 1 cup reduced sodium chicken broth
- 1 cup heavy cream (use full-fat unsweetened coconut milk for a Paleo version)
- 2 Tbsp. butter (Use coconut oil for a Paleo version)
- 3 Tbsp. Parmesan cheese, grated (eliminate for a Paleo version)
- 2 Tbsp. fresh thyme, chopped
- Salt and pepper to taste

DIRECTIONS:

1. In a food processor fitted with the shred blade, shred the cauliflower. Alternatively, you can use a cheese grater.
2. Heat the olive oil in a large pot over medium heat. Add the onion, mushrooms, carrot and garlic. Sauté for about 3 minutes, until softened.
3. Add the shredded cauliflower to the pot. Stir to combine, cover, and allow to steam for 5 minutes.
4. Increase the heat to high. Add the chicken broth and heavy cream to the pot. Season with thyme, salt and pepper.
5. Bring the mixture to a simmer and cook for about 5 minutes, until slightly thickened, stirring often.
6. Stir in the chicken and the cheese about 2 minutes before serving.

Cooking Tips: Adjust the creaminess by adding more or less cheese and heavy cream to find your perfect balance. Please note that this would affect the nutrition facts.

To make one or two servings vegetarian, simply add the cheese and then dish up the vegetarian servings before adding the chicken. Alternatively, skip the chicken and make all of the servings vegetarian.

NUTRITION FACTS (PER SERVING)

• Total Carbohydrates: 15g	% calories from:
• Dietary Fiber: 5g	
• Protein: 38g	• Fat: 53%
• Total Fat: 25g	• Carbohydrates: 14%
• Net Carbs: 10g	• Protein: 36%
• Calories: 425	

MUSHROOM CAULIFLOWER RISOTTO

GF

 Difficulty level: 2

 Cost: $$

 15 mins

 20 mins

 Serves 4

INGREDIENTS:

- 1 ½ heads cauliflower
- 3 cups fresh mushrooms, sliced
- 1 red onion, minced
- 3 cups reduced sodium chicken broth
- ¾ cup heavy cream (use full fat unsweetened coconut milk for a Paleo version)
- ¼ cup Parmesan cheese, grated (eliminate for a Paleo version)
- ¾ cup mozzarella cheese, grated (eliminate for a Paleo version)
- 3 Tbsp. butter (use coconut oil for a Paleo version)
- 1 ½ tsp. dried thyme
- Salt and pepper to taste

Cooking Tips: Try out different types of cheese to find your favorite combination.

To reheat leftovers, melt some butter in a saucepan and stir in the cold risotto.

DIRECTIONS:

1. Thoroughly wash the cauliflower, cut into florets, and place in a food processor.

2. Pulse for 2 minutes, until it resembles white rice. Alternatively, you can use a cheese grater to achieve the same result.

3. Add the butter to a saucepan and set over medium heat. Add the red onion and mushrooms and sauté for about 2 minutes.

4. Add the cauliflower, give it a stir and then pour in the broth.

5. Bring the mixture to a simmer and reduce the heat to low. Cover and cook for 5 minutes, stirring 1–2 times. When the cauliflower is al dente, remove the lid and continue cooking for another 7–10 minutes, until all the liquid has been absorbed. Watch closely that it does not burn.

6. Stir in the heavy cream, Parmesan cheese and mozzarella cheese. Season with salt, pepper and thyme, and stir well.

7. Once the cheeses are melted, remove the saucepan from the heat.

8. Serve warm.

NUTRITION FACTS (PER SERVING)

- Total Carbohydrates: 14g
- Dietary Fiber: 5g
- Protein: 24g
- Total Fat: 28g
- Net Carbs: 10g
- Calories: 385

% calories from:
- Fat: 65%
- Carbohydrates: 15%
- Protein: 25%

CHEESY "RICE"

 Difficulty level : 2

 Cost : $

 15 mins

 10-17 mins

 Serves 4

INGREDIENTS:

- 1 head cauliflower, cut into florets
- ½ cup heavy cream
- 1 cup cheddar cheese, shredded
- ½ yellow onion, finely chopped
- 1 clove garlic, chopped
- 1 tsp. dried thyme
- ¼ tsp. dried rosemary
- ½ tsp. salt
- ¼ tsp. black pepper
- Chopped green onions for serving

DIRECTIONS:

1. Start by adding the cauliflower florets to a large stockpot with enough water to cover. Bring to a boil and simmer for 5-7 minutes or until tender.

2. Drain the water and add the cauliflower to a food processor. Blend until a rice-like consistency forms.

3. Transfer the cauliflower "rice" back to the stockpot with the remaining ingredients and stir to combine.

4. Heat over a low to medium heat for 5-10 minutes or until the "rice" is heated through and the cheese has melted.

5. Top with the chopped green onions and enjoy.

NUTRITION FACTS (PER SERVING)

- Total Carbohydrates: 6g
- Dietary Fiber: 2g
- Protein: 9g
- Total Fat: 15g
- Net Carbs: 4g
- Calories: 190

- % calories from:
- Fat: 72%
- Carbohydrates: 9%
- Protein: 19%

APPLE VANILLA "RICE" PUDDING GF

Difficulty level : 1

Cost : $

15 mins

20 mins

Serves 3

INGREDIENTS:

- 1 apple, peeled and cored
- 2 eggs
- 1 cup heavy cream (use full-fat unsweetened coconut milk for a Paleo version)
- ½ tsp. cinnamon
- ¼ tsp. nutmeg
- ½ tsp. natural vanilla extract
- ½ cup coconut flakes

DIRECTIONS:

1. In a food processor fitted with the shredding disc, shred the peeled and cored apple. Alternatively, you can use a cheese grater.

2. In a medium saucepan over medium heat, add the shredded apple. Cook for about 5 minutes, until the apple begins to soften.

3. In a small bowl, whisk the heavy cream together with the eggs. Slowly add this mixture to the apple. Stir well to combine.

4. Add the coconut, cinnamon, nutmeg and vanilla extract, and stir.

5. Bring to a simmer. Allow to cook for 10 minutes, stirring often, until slightly thickened.

6. Garnish with apple slices and/or freshly grated cinnamon, if desired. Serve hot or cold.

. . . .

Cooking Tips: Adjust the amount of nutmeg and cinnamon to make it more or less sweet.

Use natural vanilla as artificial extracts will not give the recipe the same flavors.

NUTRITION FACTS (PER SERVING)

- Total Carbohydrates: 12g
- Dietary Fiber: 3g
- Protein: 5g
- Total Fat: 23g
- Net Carbs: 9g
- Calories: 265

% calories from:
- Fat: 78%
- Carbohydrates: 18%
- Protein: 8%

PIZZA

SOUTHWESTERN PIZZA GF

 Difficulty level : 2

 Cost : $$

 20 mins

 35 mins

 Serves 5

INGREDIENTS:

Crust

- 1 ½ heads cauliflower
- 3 eggs
- 1 cup Parmesan cheese
- 1 cup mozzarella cheese
- ½ tsp. salt

Fillings

- 5 Tbsp. tomato sauce
- 1 red bell pepper, sliced
- 1 green bell pepper, sliced
- ½ cup ham, chopped
- 1 ½ cups mozzarella cheese, sliced
- Fresh basil leaves

DIRECTIONS:

1. Preheat the oven to 425°F and line a pizza pan with parchment paper.

2. To prepare the crust, chop the cauliflower into florets and place in a food processor. Pulse until ground into small bits.

3. Transfer the cauliflower to a microwave-safe bowl, cover with a microwave-safe lid and microwave on high until cooked, for about 5 minutes. To prevent burning, check two or three times during the process. Allow to cool.

4. Dump the cauliflower onto a clean dishtowel or several paper towels and squeeze to remove excess moisture.

5. Transfer the drained cauliflower into a large bowl and combine with the Parmesan cheese, mozzarella cheese, eggs and salt. Mix well to combine.

6. Press the mixture into the pizza pan and bake for 20 minutes.

7. Remove the crust from the oven and allow to cool slightly.

8. Keep the oven heated to 425°F. Cover the crust with the fillings, starting with the tomato sauce.

9. Bake for about 10 minutes, until golden brown. Allow to cool for 5 minutes before serving.

NUTRITION FACTS (PER SERVING)

- Total Carbohydrates: 11g	% calories from:
- Dietary Fiber: 4g	
- Protein: 29g	- Fat: 52%
- Total Fat: 18g	- Carbohydrates: 14%
- Net Carbs: 4g	- Protein: 37%
- Calories: 310	

Cooking Tips: You can change the ham for turkey or other toppings that go well with the sweetness of bell peppers.

If you do not have a microwave, you can steam the cauliflower on the hob for about 7 minutes, or until tender, instead.

ROSEMARY & THYME
FLATBREADS (GF) (DF)

 Difficulty level : 1

 Cost : $

 15 mins

 20 mins

 Serves 3

INGREDIENTS:

- ½ cup almond flour
- 8 large egg whites
- 1 ½ tsp. gluten free baking powder (use baking soda for a Paleo version)
- 2 tsp. fresh thyme, chopped
- ¼ tsp. ground turmeric
- 3 Tbsp. fresh rosemary, chopped
- 2 Tbsp. olive oil
- ¼ tsp. salt

NUTRITION FACTS (PER SERVING)

	% calories from:
Total Carbohydrates: 10g	
Dietary Fiber: 5g	Fat: 69%
Protein: 16g	Carbohydrates: 13%
Total Fat: 23g	Protein: 21%
Net Carbs: 5g	
Calories: 300	

DIRECTIONS:

1. In a blender or food processor, combine all of the ingredients, except for the olive oil, and blend until well combined.

2. In a large frying pan, heat about a third of the olive oil over medium heat.

3. Pour one third of the mixture into the frying pan and allow to cook for about 3 minutes, until bubbles start to appear. Carefully flip and continue cooking for an additional 3 minutes.

4. Remove the flatbread from the pan and repeat with the remaining batter.

Cooking Tips: Swap the rosemary for other herbs like dill or thyme.

It is important to wait for the frying pan to heat up before pouring the mixture into the pan as this helps to create the crust.

Serving Suggestions: The flatbreads can be enjoyed on their own, alongside your entrée or used as a pizza base.

44

HAM AND CHEESE
PIZZA ROLLS
GF

 Difficulty level : 2

 Cost : $$

 15 mins

 30 mins

 Serves 5

INGREDIENTS:

Dough

- ½ cup Parmesan cheese
- 1 cup mozzarella cheese
- 3 egg whites
- ¾ cup coconut flour
- 1 cup heavy cream

Filling

- 2 cups of cooked ham, sliced
- 1 cup Gouda cheese, sliced
- 5 Tbsp. tomato sauce
- 1 tsp. crushed black pepper for topping

DIRECTIONS:

1. Preheat the oven to 400°F and line a baking sheet with parchment paper.

2. In a food processor, combine the ingredients for the crust and process until a smooth dough is formed. You may need to add water, one tablespoon at a time, to achieve this result.

3. Flatten the dough into a rectangular shape onto the prepared baking sheet. Bake for about 15 minutes. Remove from the oven and allow to cool slightly.

4. Spread the tomato sauce evenly across the dough. Top with the sliced ham and Gouda cheese.

5. Carefully roll the dough into a log. Slice the log into 5 even pieces and place each one back onto the baking sheet. Sprinkle with crushed black pepper.

6. Bake again for about 10 minutes, until the dough is golden brown and the cheese is bubbly.

NUTRITION FACTS (PER SERVING)

• Total Carbohydrates: 6g	% calories from:
• Dietary Fiber: 2g	• Fat: 64%
• Protein: 35g	• Carbohydrates: 5%
• Total Fat:35g	• Protein: 28%
• Net Carbs: 4g	
• Calories: 492	

Cooking Tip: After the first baking, the dough should be soft but dry. Wait for the dough to cool down a bit before rolling as this helps prevent the dough from falling apart.

SPINACH AND MOZARELLA PIZZA GF

 Difficulty level : 2

 Cost : $$

 15 mins

 25 mins

 Serves 5

INGREDIENTS:

Dough

- 1 ½ cups almond flour
- 4 eggs
- ¼ cup water
- 1 tsp. gluten free baking powder
- 3 Tbsp. olive oil
- 1 tsp. butter, melted
- Pinch of salt

Toppings

- 1 (8-ounce) package frozen spinach, thawed and drained
- 3 cups mozzarella cheese, grated
- 3 garlic cloves, minced

DIRECTIONS:

1. Preheat the oven to 425°F.

2. Place the almond flour into a food processor with the water, eggs, olive oil, gluten free baking powder and salt.

3. Process until smooth. Pour the butter into the bottom of a 9" cake pan. Pour the batter on top and spread it out evenly.

4. Bake for 15 minutes. Remove from the oven and allow to cool slightly. Carefully flip the crust onto a baking sheet lined with parchment paper.

5. Spread the garlic onto the crust and evenly distribute the spinach on top. Then, sprinkle with the mozzarella cheese.

6. Place back in the oven for 15 minutes, until the crust is golden and the cheese is bubbly.

Cooking Tips: You can add herbs and spices to the dough to create limitless flavor combinations.

Get creative with the toppings! Mix minced garlic with a few tablespoons of tomato paste, change half the mozzarella for cheddar and sprinkle some oregano on top. Create your own pizza.

NUTRITION FACTS (PER SERVING)	
• Total Carbohydrates: 9g	% calories from:
• Dietary Fiber: 3g	
• Protein: 26g	• Fat: 76%
• Total Fat:42g	• Carbohydrates: 7%
• Net Carbs: 6g	• Protein: 21%
• Calories: 500	

FOUR CHEESE PIZZA

GF

INGREDIENTS:

- Dough
- 2 heads cauliflower
- 5 eggs
- 1 ½ cup Parmesan cheese
- 2 cups mozzarella cheese
- 1 tsp. salt
- ½ tsp. curry powder
- 1 tsp. fresh thyme, chopped
- Toppings
- ¾ cup tomato sauce
- 1 cup mozzarella cheese, grated
- ¼ cup Gouda cheese, grated
- 2 tomatoes, thinly sliced
- ¼ cup fresh basil, roughly chopped

. . . .

Cooking Tips: Drizzle with olive oil before baking for the second time as this helps to release the flavors.

Get creative and adjust the toppings as desired.

DIRECTIONS:

1. Preheat the oven to 425°F and line a large pizza pan with parchment paper.

2. To prepare the crust, chop the cauliflower into florets and place in a food processor. Pulse until ground into small bits.

3. Transfer the cauliflower to a microwave-safe bowl, cover with a microwave-safe lid and microwave on high for about 3 minutes or until cooked. Allow to cool.

4. Dump the cauliflower onto a clean dish towel or several paper towels and squeeze to remove excess moisture.

5. Transfer the drained cauliflower into a large bowl and combine with the Parmesan cheese, mozzarella cheese, curry, thyme, eggs and salt. Mix well to combine.

6. Press the mixture into the prepared pizza pan and bake for about 20 minutes.

7. Remove the pizza base from the oven and allow to cool slightly.

8. Spread the sauce onto the crust evenly. Sprinkle with the cheeses and top with the sliced tomatoes and basil.

9. Return to the oven for 10 minutes, or until the cheese layer is bubbly and the crust is golden brown around the edges.

10. Slice and serve.

NUTRITION FACTS (PER SERVING)	
• Total Carbohydrates: 12g	% calories from:
• Dietary Fiber: 3g	• Fat: 58%
• Protein: 38g	• Carbohydrates: 11%
• Total Fat:27g	• Protein: 36%
• Net Carbs: 9g	
• Calories: 420	

QUICHES & SAVORY PIES

CARAMELIZED ONION & GARLIC TART **GF**

 Difficulty level : 3

 Cost : $$

 30 mins

 45 mins

 Serves 10

INGREDIENTS:

Crust

- 2 cups almond flour
- ¾ cup butter
- 4 egg whites
- 1 pinch salt

Filling

- 2 cups mozzarella cheese, grated
- 3 onions, thinly sliced
- 5 garlic cloves, minced
- 1 Tbsp. lemon juice
- 5 eggs, beaten
- 3 Tbsp. fresh basil, chopped
- 2 tsp. dried thyme
- 1 tsp. dried parsley
- 5 Tbsp. olive oil
- Salt and pepper to taste

Cooking Tips: The crust mixture should resemble coarse meal and stick together when squeezed. If needed, add water or almond flour, one tablespoon at a time, until proper consistency is reached.

Experiment a little with different herbs and spices in the filling.

DIRECTIONS:

1. Preheat the oven to 350°F and grease a tart pan.

2. In a large bowl, prepare the crust by mixing the flour together with the egg whites, salt and butter with your hands until well combined.

3. Press the mixture into the bottom and sides of the greased tart pan.

4. To prepare the filling, heat the olive oil in a large frying pan over medium heat. Add the onion and cook for about 5 minutes, until softened. Season with salt and pepper.

5. Add the garlic, reduce the heat to low and continue cooking for 2 minutes, stirring frequently to prevent burning.

6. Stir in the lemon juice and cook for another 5 minutes.

7. Transfer the onions into the prepared tart pan and top with the beaten eggs, basil, thyme, parsley and shredded cheese.

8. Bake for about 20 minutes, until the eggs are set.

9. Allow to cool for 10 minutes before serving. Enjoy!

NUTRITION FACTS (PER SERVING)

- Total Carbohydrates: 9g
- Dietary Fiber: 3g
- Protein: 15g
- Total Fat: 37g
- Net Carbs: 6g
- Calories: 411

% calories from:
- Fat: 81%
- Carbohydrates: 9%
- Protein: 15%

SHEPHERD'S PIE

GF

Difficulty level : 1

$ Cost: $$$

15 mins

30 mins

Serves 6

INGREDIENTS:

Bottom Layer:

- 1 ½ pound ground beef
- 1 red onion, chopped
- 2 cloves garlic, minced
- 3 tomatoes, chopped
- ½ cup frozen peas (eliminate for a Paleo version)
- 1 cup reduced sodium beef stock
- ½ tsp. ground cumin
- 2 Tbsp. olive oil
- Salt and pepper to taste

Top Layer:

- 1 ½ heads cauliflower, cut into florets
- ½ cup heavy cream (use full fat unsweetened coconut milk for a Paleo version)
- ¼ cup Parmesan cheese, grated (eliminate for a Paleo version)
- ¼ tsp. curry powder
- 5 Tbsp. fresh chives, finely chopped
- 3 Tbsp. butter (use coconut oil for a Paleo version)
- Salt and pepper to taste

Cooking Tip: Simmer the mixture with the ground beef until almost dry. This helps to concentrate the flavors and avoid the pie getting too wet.

DIRECTIONS:

1. In a large pot, steam the cauliflower for about 10 minutes, until tender.

2. Drain and return to the pot. Add the butter, heavy cream, curry powder and cheese. Season with salt and pepper.

3. Purée the cauliflower using an immersion blender. Alternatively, it can be puréed in a food processor. Set aside.

4. Add the olive oil to a large frying pan over medium heat. Sauté the onion and garlic for about 3 minutes, then add in the peas and tomatoes. Cook over low heat for about 5 minutes.

5. Add the ground beef and cook until browned.

6. Stir in the stock and cumin. Season with salt and pepper. Simmer until most of the liquid has evaporated.

7. Preheat the oven's broiler and distribute the filling evenly in a baking dish, and top with the pureed cauliflower.

8. Place under the broiler for about 5 minutes, until golden brown.

9. Sprinkle with fresh chives and serve straightaway.

NUTRITION FACTS (PER SERVING)

- Total Carbohydrates: 11g
- Dietary Fiber: 4g
- Protein: 41g
- Total Fat: 23g
- Net Carbs: 7g
- Calories: 415

% calories from:
- Fat: 50%
- Carbohydrates: 11%
- Protein: 40%

SPINACH AND MUSHROOM CRUSTLESS QUICHE (GF)

 Difficulty level : 1

 Cost : $

 15 mins

 35 mins

 Serves 3

INGREDIENTS:

- 4 cups fresh spinach leaves
- 1 cup of white mushrooms, thinly sliced
- 2 cloves garlic, chopped
- 8 large eggs
- ½ cup heavy cream
- 1 cup Gouda cheese, diced
- 10 sprigs fresh parsley, chopped
- 2 Tbsp. fresh cilantro, chopped
- 2 tsp. fresh thyme
- 1 tsp. ground nutmeg
- 2 Tbsp. olive oil
- Salt and pepper to taste

DIRECTIONS:

1. Preheat the oven to 375°F. Prepare a 9" pie dish with non-stick cooking spray.

2. Heat the olive oil in a large frying pan over medium heat.

3. Add the mushrooms and garlic to the pan and sauté for about 5 minutes, until golden brown. Remove from the heat.

4. In a large bowl, whisk the eggs together with the heavy cream.

5. Stir in the spinach, parsley, cilantro, thyme, cooked mushrooms, nutmeg and Gouda cheese. Season with salt and pepper.

6. Transfer the mixture to the prepared pie dish and bake for about 30 minutes, until the eggs are set and golden around the edges.

7. Allow to cool for 10 minutes before slicing.

Cooking Tips: Try adding kale and mushrooms or combining more cheeses.

NUTRITION FACTS (PER SERVING)

- Total Carbohydrates: 6g
- Dietary Fiber: 1g
- Protein: 29g
- Total Fat: 48g
- Net Carbs: 5g
- Calories: 563

% calories from:
- Fat: 77%
- Carbohydrates: 4%
- Protein: 21%

BACON, EGG AND CHEESE QUICHE GF

 Difficulty level : 2

 Cost : $$

 15 mins

 40 mins

 Serves 8

INGREDIENTS:

Crust
- ¼ cup coconut flour
- 2 cups almond flour
- 3 Tbsp. whole milk
- 3 egg whites
- ½ cup butter
- 1 pinch nutmeg

Filling
- 8 eggs
- 6 slices bacon, cooked and crumbled
- 2 cups mozzarella cheese, grated
- 2 garlic cloves, chopped
- ½ of a white onion, chopped
- 1 tsp. fresh oregano, chopped
- 1 Tbsp. Italian seasoning

Cooking Tip: After removing the crust mixture from the food processor, you may need to add a bit more coconut flour before pressing it into the pie pan, if the dough is too moist.

DIRECTIONS:

1. Preheat the oven to 375°F and lightly grease a 9" pie pan.

2. To prepare the crust, add the flours to a food processor and pulse several times to remove any clumps.

3. In another bowl, whisk together the egg whites, nutmeg and milk.

4. Add the butter to the food processor and pulse until the butter is broken into small clumps. With the food processor on low, slowly stream in the egg/water mixture until the dough forms into a ball. Add more milk if needed.

5. Press the mixture into the prepared pie pan and refrigerate for at least 30 minutes.

6. To prepare the filling, whisk the eggs in a large bowl until frothy.

7. Stir in the bacon, oregano, Italian seasoning, garlic, onion and cheese, and mix well. Pour into the prepared pie crust and bake for approximately 30 minutes, until the eggs are set and the crust is golden brown.

8. Allow to cool for about 10 minutes before slicing.

NUTRITION FACTS (PER SERVING)

- Total Carbohydrates: 11g
- Dietary Fiber: 5g
- Protein: 22g
- Total Fat: 39g
- Net Carbs: 6g
- Calories: 468

% calories from:
- Fat: 75%
- Carbohydrates: 9%
- Protein: 19%

BEEF POT PIE

GF

Difficulty level : 2

Cost : $$$

35 mins

30 mins

Serves 6

INGREDIENTS:

Crust
- ¼ cup coconut flour
- 2 cups almond flour
- ¾ cup butter, hard
- 8 Tbsp. cold water
- ½ tsp. gluten free baking powder
- 1 pinch of salt

Filling
- 1 ½ pound ground beef
- 1 onion, diced
- 3 cloves garlic, minced
- 1 cup reduced sodium beef broth
- ¾ cup heavy cream
- ½ cup Parmesan cheese, cubed
- ½ cup mozzarella cheese, grated
- ½ tsp. garlic powder
- 3 Tbsp. olive oil
- Salt and pepper to taste

NUTRITION FACTS (PER SERVING)	
• Total Carbohydrates: 11g	% calories from:
• Dietary Fiber: 5g	
• Protein: 49g	• Fat: 72%
• Total Fat: 64g	• Carbohydrates: 6%
• Net Carbs: 7g	• Protein: 25%
• Calories: 800	

DIRECTIONS:

1. To prepare the crust, add the flours, salt and gluten free baking powder to a food processor and pulse several times to remove any clumps.

2. Add the butter and pulse 10–15 times, until the mixture resembles coarse sand. With the food processor running, slowly stream the cold water in until the dough forms into a ball.

3. Transfer the dough to wax paper and flatten into a disc about 9" in diameter. Refrigerate for 30 minutes.

4. Preheat the oven to 350°F.

5. Heat the olive oil in a large frying pan over medium heat. Add the onion and garlic to the frying pan and cook for about 3 minutes.

6. Add the ground beef and season with salt and pepper. Cook until the ground beef is browned.

7. Slowly stir in the beef stock and heavy cream. Add the garlic powder and mix well.

8. Reduce the heat to low and allow to simmer for 10 minutes, until slightly thickened.

9. Transfer the mixture to a 9" pie dish. Top with the chilled crust and cheeses. Bake for about 30 minutes, until the crust is golden brown and the filling is bubbly.

10. Allow to cool for 5 minutes before serving.

Cooking Tips: You may need to add more coconut flour after removing the dough from the food processor, if the dough is too moist. Add just one tablespoon at a time.

Adapt this recipe by swapping the beef and beef broth for cubed chicken breast and chicken broth, or make a vegetarian version with mushrooms and vegetable broth.

NOODLES & PASTA

STUFFED SPAGHETTI SQUASH (GF)

 Difficulty level : 2

 Cost : $$

 15 mins

 90 mins

Serves 3

INGREDIENTS:

- ½ pound ground beef
- 1 spaghetti squash
- 1 small onion, minced
- 2 fresh tomatoes, chopped
- 2 tsp. fresh oregano, chopped
- ½ cup mozzarella cheese, grated (eliminate for a Paleo version)
- 3 Tbsp. olive oil
- 1 tsp. garlic powder
- Salt and pepper to taste

DIRECTIONS:

1. Preheat the oven to 375°F and grease a baking pan.

2. Cut your spaghetti squash in half lengthwise and scoop out the seeds. Place cut side down on the baking pan, cover with aluminum foil and bake for about 80 minutes, until fork tender.

3. Meanwhile, heat the olive oil in a large skillet over medium heat. Add the ground beef and cook until browned.

4. Stir in the onion and cook for about 3 minutes. Then add garlic powder, tomatoes and spices. Cook for 2–3 minutes, until heated through.

5. Reduce the heat to low. Using a fork, shred the spaghetti squash flesh into strands. Add to the pan and mix well.

6. Divide the mixture evenly between the two squash shells. Top with shredded mozzarella and bake for about 10 minutes, until cheese is melted and bubbly.

NUTRITION FACTS (PER SERVING)

- Total Carbohydrates: 11g
- Dietary Fiber: 2g
- Protein: 30g
- Total Fat: 23g
- Net Carbs: 9g
- Calories: 360

% calories from:
- Fat: 58%
- Carbohydrates: 12%
- Protein: 33%

Cooking Tip: The baking time of the squash can vary so increase or reduce the time as needed. The most important thing is being able to shred the squash.

ZUCCHINI NOODLE SHRIMP

GF

 Difficulty level : 2

 Cost : $$$

 10 mins

 15 mins

 Serves 5

INGREDIENTS:

- 3 large zucchinis, spiralized or cut into thin ribbons
- 1 ½ pounds shrimp, shelled and deveined
- 3 garlic cloves, minced
- ¾ cup dry white wine
- 1 lemon, juiced
- 3 Tbsp. butter (use coconut oil for a Paleo version)
- ¼ tsp. cumin
- 1 tsp. dried oregano
- 1 tsp. garlic powder
- Salt and pepper to taste

Cooking Tip: The butter should be hot enough to brown the shrimp, otherwise the shrimp will release juices and the texture will not be the best.

DIRECTIONS:

1. Heat half of the butter in a large skillet over medium heat.

2. Add the garlic and cook for 1 minute, until softened. Remove from pan and set aside.

3. Heat the remaining butter, add the shrimp and cook for 3 minutes, or until pink throughout.

4. Remove the shrimp from the pan and increase the heat to medium-high. Add the white wine and lemon juice to the pan and stir well to remove any of the browned bits from the bottom of the pan.

5. Add the zucchini noodles and season with cumin, dried oregano, garlic powder, salt and pepper. Cook for about 3 minutes, stirring occasionally.

6. Transfer the shrimp back to the pan and toss well to combine. Enjoy!

NUTRITION FACTS (PER SERVING)

- Total Carbohydrates: 8g
- Dietary Fiber: 2g
- Protein: 20g
- Total Fat: 9g
- Net Carbs: 6g
- Calories: 215

% calories from:
- Fat: 38%
- Carbohydrates: 15%
- Protein: 37%

GARLIC SPAGHETTI SQUASH
WITH PARMESAN GF

Difficulty level : 2

Cost : $$

20 mins

90 mins

Serves 2

INGREDIENTS:

- 1 spaghetti squash, seeded and cut in half lengthwise
- 3 garlic cloves, minced
- ¼ cup reduced sodium chicken broth
- 2 egg yolks
- ¾ cup Parmesan cheese, grated (eliminate for a Paleo version)
- 4 Tbsp. butter (use coconut oil for a Paleo version)
- 3 Tbsp. fresh sage leaves
- Salt and pepper to taste

DIRECTIONS:

1. Preheat the oven to 375°F. Season the spaghetti squash halves with salt and pepper and place cut side down in a large baking dish. Bake for about 80 minutes, until fork tender. Remove from the oven and allow to cool.

2. Once cooled, shred the squash with a fork and transfer to a large bowl.

3. In a large skillet over medium heat, melt the butter.

4. Add the garlic and sage, and sauté for 1 minute. Stir in the chicken broth and bring to a boil over low heat.

5. In a small bowl, whisk the eggs together with the Parmesan cheese. Season with salt and pepper.

6. Add the eggs to the pan and immediately follow with the spaghetti squash. Do not allow the eggs to scramble.

7. Toss well to combine. Allow everything to heat through and thicken a bit.

8. Serve immediately.

. . . .

Cooking Tip: Add more garlic if you like stronger flavors.

Serving Suggestion: Garnish with additional Parmesan cheese and fresh sage, if desired.

NUTRITION FACTS (PER SERVING)

- Total Carbohydrates: 11g
- Dietary Fiber: 1g
- Protein: 14g
- Total Fat: 27g
- Net Carbs: 10g
- Calories: 325

% calories from:
- Fat: 75%
- Carbohydrates: 14%
- Protein: 17%

HERBS & RICOTTA
STUFFED ZUCCHINI GF

 Difficulty level : 2

 Cost : $$

 15 mins

 30 mins

Serves 3

INGREDIENTS:

- ¾ cup ricotta cheese
- ½ cup sour cream
- 4 Tbsp. Parmesan cheese
- ¼ tsp. garlic powder
- 1 tsp. fresh oregano, chopped
- 4 Tbsp. fresh basil, chopped
- 1 tsp. fresh dill, chopped
- 2 large zucchinis, cut lengthwise into very thin slices
- 4 sun-dried tomatoes, finely chopped
- 4 Tbsp. olive oil
- Salt and pepper to taste

DIRECTIONS:

1. Preheat the oven to 375°F. Grease a baking dish with olive oil.

2. In a blender or food processor, blend the ricotta, sour cream, Parmesan cheese, spices and herbs until smooth and creamy.

3. Brush each zucchini slice with a bit of olive oil and season with black pepper. Grill or sauté the slices for about 2 minutes per side, until soft and pliable.

4. Spoon about a tablespoon of the cheese mixture onto one side of a zucchini slice in an even layer. Sprinkle with some of the sun-dried tomatoes. Roll up and place seam-side down into the prepared baking dish.

5. Repeat with the remaining zucchini, cheese mixture and tomatoes.

6. Drizzle the zucchini rolls with the remaining olive oil and sprinkle with black pepper.

7. Bake for about 25 minutes until the cheese is bubbly and melted.

8. Serve immediately.

NUTRITION FACTS (PER SERVING)

- Total Carbohydrates: 8g
- Dietary Fiber: 1g
- Protein: 20g
- Total Fat: 26g
- Net Carbs: 7g
- Calories: 336

% calories from:
- Fat: 70%
- Carbohydrates: 10%
- Protein: 24%

Cooking Tips: For some variety, replace ricotta with other cheeses and add more sour cream, if desired.

The zucchini slices should be thin, but you should be able to create a roll.

Soak the sun-dried tomatoes in warm water for about 15 minutes if they are hard to chop.

ITALIAN LASAGNA

GF

Difficulty level : 3

Cost : $$$

20 mins

50 mins

Serves 5

INGREDIENTS:

- 1lb ground turkey
- 2 medium zucchinis
- 1 cup marinara sauce
- 2 cups mozzarella cheese, sliced
- ¼ cup Parmesan cheese, grated
- 1 small onion, diced
- 3 garlic cloves, minced
- 1 egg
- 1 Tbsp. crushed red pepper (adjust to taste)
- 2 tsp. fresh oregano, chopped
- 2 Tbsp. heavy cream
- 2 Tbsp. olive oil
- Salt and pepper to taste
- Fresh basil and thyme (optional garnish)

. . . .

Cooking Tip: To prevent the zucchinis from releasing too much water in the oven, dry each slice before searing it in the skillet. Sprinkle some salt over the slices (on both sides) and let them rest for about 15 minutes. Then dry with paper towel and remove the salt.

NUTRITION FACTS (PER SERVING)

• Total Carbohydrates: 13g	% calories from:
• Dietary Fiber: 4g	• Fat: 57%
• Protein: 43g	• Carbohydrates: 11%
• Total Fat: 30g	• Protein: 37%
• Net Carbs: 9g	
• Calories: 470	

DIRECTIONS:

1. Preheat the oven to 350°F. Prepare a baking dish with non-stick cooking spray.

2. Using a mandolin or very sharp knife, slice the zucchinis lengthwise into 1/8 inch (3mm) thick slices.

3. Heat the olive oil in a large skillet over medium-high heat. Working in batches so as to not overload the pan, sear the zucchini slices, about 2 minutes on each side. Set aside.

4. In the same pan, sauté the onion and garlic with the ground turkey. Season with the oregano, crushed red pepper, salt and pepper. Continue to sauté until cooked through and browned. Remove from the heat and allow to cool slightly.

5. In a small bowl, whisk together the egg and heavy cream until smooth.

6. To assemble the lasagna, layer a couple of spoonfuls of marinara into the bottom of the baking dish. Top with a layer of the zucchini slices. Evenly spread about a third of the egg mixture, followed by about a third of the turkey mixture. Top with a third of the mozzarella cheese. Repeat twice with the remaining ingredients.

7. Top with any remaining zucchini slices and evenly sprinkle the Parmesan cheese over everything.

8. Cover with foil and bake for 30 minutes. Remove the foil and continue baking for 20 minutes.

9. Garnish with fresh herbs, if desired. Allow to cool for 5 minutes prior to serving.

GARLICKY EGG NOODLES GF

 Difficulty level : 2

 Cost : $

 15 mins

 3-5 mins

 Serves 2

INGREDIENTS:

- 2 eggs at room temperature
- 2 Tbsp. cream cheese
- ½ tsp. garlic powder
- ½ tsp. onion powder
- Pinch of salt and pepper

Cooking Tip: It is best to use a silicone mat as this will help these fragile noodles from sticking to the baking sheet.

DIRECTIONS:

1. Start by preheating the oven to 300°F and lining a baking sheet with a non-stick silicone mat.

2. While the oven is heating, add the ingredients to the base of a food processor or high-speed blender and blend.

3. Pour the mixture on top of the baking sheet and smooth with a silicone spatula.

4. Place in the oven and bake for 3-5 minutes, being sure not to burn the noodles!

5. Allow them to cool for 2-3 minutes and then slice into noodle shapes.

6. Serve with your sauce of choice.

NUTRITION FACTS (PER SERVING)

- Total Carbohydrates: 2g
- Dietary Fiber: 0g
- Protein: 7g
- Total Fat: 8g
- Net Carbs: 2g
- Calories: 102

% calories from:
- Fat: 67%
- Carbohydrates: 7%
- Protein: 26%

BREAKFASTS

VANILLA MAPLE BELGIAN
WAFFLES GF

 Difficulty level : 1

 Cost : $$

 15 mins

 10 mins

 Serves 4

INGREDIENTS:

- ¼ cup coconut flour
- ½ cup almond flour
- ½ cup butter, melted (use coconut oil for a Paleo version)
- ¼ cup heavy whipping cream (use full fat unsweetened coconut milk for a Paleo version)
- 6 eggs
- 1 tsp. erythritol (use pure grade B maple syrup for a Paleo version)
- ½ tsp. pure vanilla extract
- ½ tsp. sugar free maple extract (eliminate for a Paleo version)
- 2 tsp. ground cinnamon
- ½ tsp. gluten free baking powder (use baking soda for a Paleo version)
- ¼ tsp. salt
- ½ cup fresh berries

DIRECTIONS:

1. In a blender or food processor, mix the eggs, maple extract and vanilla with the butter until well combined.

2. Add the erythritol, gluten free baking powder, cinnamon, salt, almond flour and coconut flour. Blend until smooth.

3. Allow the batter to rest for at least 5 minutes to thicken.

4. Whip the heavy cream until stiff peaks form. Set aside.

5. Spray a waffle maker with non-stick spray and pour quarter of the batter into it. Follow the manufacturer's recommendation for cooking time and repeat with the remaining batter until done.

6. Top the waffles with the fresh whipped cream and berries. Enjoy!

Cooking Tip: Wait for the waffle maker to heat up before pouring in the batter as this helps to create the beautiful brown crust.

NUTRITION FACTS (PER SERVING)

- Total Carbohydrates: 13g
- Dietary Fiber: 5g
- Protein: 13g
- Total Fat: 43g
- Net Carbs: 8g
- Calories: 475

% calories from:
- Fat: 81%
- Carbohydrates: 11%
- Protein: 11%

ALMOND PANCAKES WITH STRAWBERRY SAUCE

GF

 Difficulty level : 2

 Cost : $$

 15 mins

🕐 10 mins

🍽 Serves 2

INGREDIENTS:

Strawberry Sauce

- ½ cup fresh strawberries, chopped
- 1 Tbsp. raw stevia
- 2 Tbsp. water
- 2 Tbsp. lemon juice

Almond Pancakes

- 4 large eggs
- ½ cup almond flour
- ¼ cup sliced almonds
- ¼ cup butter, melted (use coconut oil for a Paleo version)
- 1 Tbsp. raw stevia
- ¼ tsp. gluten free baking powder (use baking soda for a Paleo version)

DIRECTIONS:

1. To prepare the strawberry sauce, blend the strawberries, water and lemon juice in a blender and transfer to a small saucepan. Cook over low heat until thickened. Allow to cool down. Then, stir in 1 tablespoon of stevia and set aside.

2. In a medium bowl, whisk the eggs together until fluffy.

3. In a separate bowl, mix almond flour, 1 tablespoon of stevia and gluten free baking powder until well combined.

4. Stir in half of the melted butter into the eggs, reserving the other half of the butter to grease the pan.

5. Add the dry ingredients to the wet and mix well.

6. Grease a large frying pan with the remaining butter and spoon 2 small pancakes for every serving.

7. Cook over low heat for about 5 minutes until the pancake starts to firm up. Flip and cook the other side for about a minute.

8. Remove from frying pan, cover with foil to keep warm and repeat with remaining batter.

9. Top the pancakes with the strawberry sauce, sprinkle with sliced almonds and serve!

. . . .

Cooking Tip: Add a splash of water or milk if the batter seems too thick, although it should be a bit thicker than regular pancake batter.

NUTRITION FACTS (PER SERVING)

- Total Carbohydrates: 12g
- Dietary Fiber: 5g
- Protein: 21g
- Total Fat: 51g
- Net Carbs: 7g
- Calories: 570

% calories from:
- Fat: 81%
- Carbohydrates: 8%
- Protein: 15%

CHOCOLATE-FILLED CRÊPES (GF)

 Difficulty level : 2

 Cost : $

 10 mins

 10 mins

 Serves 4

INGREDIENTS:

Crepes

- 3 eggs, beaten
- ¼ cup whole milk (use full fat unsweetened coconut milk for a Paleo version)
- 1 tsp. raw stevia
- ½ tsp. natural vanilla extract
- ½ cup almond flour
- ¼ tsp. gluten free baking powder (use baking soda for a Paleo version)
- ¼ tsp. baking soda
- 1 pinch salt
- Butter for greasing (use coconut oil for a Paleo version)

Chocolate Filling

- ½ cup heavy cream (use full fat unsweetened coconut milk for a Paleo version)
- 4 Tbsp. unsweetened raw cocoa powder
- 2 tsp. raw stevia

DIRECTIONS:

1. In a small bowl, mix all the filling ingredients and set aside.

2. To prepare the crêpes, whisk together the eggs, milk, stevia, salt and vanilla extract.

3. Slowly whisk in the almond flour, gluten free baking powder and baking soda until well combined.

4. Grease a medium frying pan with butter and place over medium heat. Once the pan is hot, ladle a small amount of the mixture into the pan and swirl to create a thin crêpe.

5. Once bubbles begin to surface, carefully flip and cook for about 1 minute on the opposite side.

6. Remove from the pan and repeat with the remaining mixture.

7. In a small saucepan, heat the chocolate mixture until warmed. Spread a thin layer onto each crêpe and then roll the crêpe up. Serve immediately!

Cooking Tip: Add more cocoa powder if you would prefer a dark chocolate filling.

NUTRITION FACTS (PER SERVING)

- Total Carbohydrates: 10g
- Dietary Fiber: 3g
- Protein: 9g
- Total Fat: 22g
- Net Carbs: 7g
- Calories: 255

% calories from:
- Fat:78%
- Carbohydrates: 16%
- Protein:14%

SWEET POTATO & SAUSAGE HASH WITH EGGS GF

 Difficulty level : 1

 Cost : $$

 10 mins

 25 mins

 Serves 3

INGREDIENTS:

- 15 ounces breakfast sausage, sliced
- 1 sweet potato, diced
- 1 red onion, chopped
- 2 garlic cloves, minced
- 3 eggs
- Fresh thyme, chopped
- 2 Tbsp. butter
- Salt and pepper to taste

DIRECTIONS:

1. In a large skillet, melt the butter, add the sausage and cook over medium heat until browned.

2. Remove the cooked sausage from the pan, leaving any rendered grease in the skillet.

3. Increase the heat to high and add the sweet potato, garlic and onion to the skillet. Cook for about 5 minutes, stirring often to prevent sticking.

4. Transfer the sausage back to the pan and cook for another 3 minutes.

5. Make three wells in the mixture and carefully crack the eggs into the wells.

6. Reduce the heat to low, cover, and cook for 3–5 minutes, until eggs are done to your liking.

7. Season with salt, pepper and thyme to taste.

Cooking Tips: Do not stir the mixture after placing the eggs in the skillet. Just reduce the heat and let them cook.

Try replacing the sausage with fresh ground beef.

NUTRITION FACTS (PER SERVING)

- Total Carbohydrates: 12g
- Dietary Fiber: 2g
- Protein: 21g
- Total Fat: 32g
- Net Carbs: 10g
- Calories: 420

% calories from:
- Fat: 69%
- Carbohydrates: 11%
- Protein: 20%

SPINACH AND GOUDA EGG MUFFINS GF

 Difficulty level : 1

 Cost : $$

 15 mins

 20 mins

 Serves 3

INGREDIENTS:

- 5 large eggs
- 2 cups baby spinach, chopped
- 2 cloves garlic, minced
- ¾ cup Gouda cheese, diced
- 3 Tbsp. heavy cream
- 2 Tbsp. olive oil
- ½ Tbsp. gluten free baking powder
- 1 tsp. dried thyme
- 1 tsp. dried oregano
- Salt and pepper to taste

DIRECTIONS:

1. Preheat the oven to 350°F. Prepare a 6-cavity muffin tin with paper liners.

2. Heat the olive oil in a large skillet over medium heat. Add the baby spinach and minced garlic. Cook for about 3 minutes, until the spinach is wilted and the garlic is golden brown. Remove from the heat.

3. In a large bowl, whisk the eggs and gluten free baking powder until frothy.

4. Stir in the heavy cream, Gouda cheese, thyme, oregano and spinach. Season with salt and pepper.

5. Evenly divide the mixture between the muffin cups.

6. Bake for 18–20 minutes, until the eggs are set and slightly brown.

7. Allow to cool for 10 minutes before removing from the pan.

8. Enjoy immediately or store in an airtight container in the fridge.

NUTRITION FACTS (PER SERVING)

- Total Carbohydrates: 4g
- Dietary Fiber: 1g
- Protein: 19g
- Total Fat: 31g
- Net Carbs: 3g
- Calories: 363

% calories from:
- Fat: 77%
- Carbohydrates: 4%
- Protein: 21%

Cooking Tip: Before adding spinach to the mixture, press the leaves to remove any water excess.

DEVILS FOOD DONUTS

GF DF

 Difficulty level : 2

 Cost : $

 10 mins

 15-20 mins

 Serves 8

INGREDIENTS:

- ¼ cup coconut flour, sifted
- 2 Tbsp. almond flour
- ¼ cup erythritol
- 1 tsp. baking powder
- ¼ cup raw unsweetened cocoa powder
- 5 eggs
- ¼ cup coconut oil, melted + more for greasing
- 1 tsp. pure vanilla extract

DIRECTIONS:

1. Start by preheating the oven to 300°F and greasing a donut pan with coconut oil.

2. Add the coconut flour, erythritol, cocoa powder and baking powder to a large mixing bowl, and stir well.

3. Add in the remaining ingredients and whisk to combine.

4. Pour the batter into the donut pan and bake for 15-20 minutes or until the donuts are set and firm to touch.

5. Allow them to cool for 5 minutes before removing.

NUTRITION FACTS (PER SERVING)

- Total Carbohydrates: 15g
- Dietary Fiber: 4g
- Protein: 5g
- Total Fat: 12g
- Net Carbs: 11g
- Calories: 146

% calories from:
- Fat: 63%
- Carbohydrates: 11%
- Protein: 5%

SNACKS

BEAN FREE "HUMMUS" GF

 Difficulty level : 1

 Cost : $

 10 minutes (plus time in fridge)

 10 minutes

 Serves 4

INGREDIENTS:

- 1 zucchini, seeded and chopped
- 3 cups cauliflower florets
- 4 Tbsp. tahini
- 3 Tbsp. lemon juice
- 2 cloves garlic
- 1 tsp. smoked paprika
- 3 Tbsp. olive oil
- ¼ cup heavy cream (use full fat unsweetened coconut milk for a Paleo version)
- 1 Tbsp. butter (use coconut oil for a Paleo version)
- Salt and pepper to taste

DIRECTIONS:

1. Heat the butter in a saucepan and add the cauliflower. Sauté until tender.

2. Place the cooked cauliflower and all of the remaining ingredients in a blender or food processor and blend on high about 2 minutes, until smooth and creamy.

3. If the mixture is too thick, add a bit of water until desired consistency is reached.

4. Transfer to a serving bowl, cover and refrigerate for at least 30 minutes.

5. Serve alongside fresh vegetables such as carrots, celery and broccoli.

Cooking Tip: Adjust the tahini amount according to your preference.

Serving Suggestion: Serve with the "5 MINUTE NAAN BREAD"

NUTRITION FACTS (PER SERVING)

- Total Carbohydrates: 10g
- Dietary Fiber: 4g
- Protein: 5g
- Total Fat: 25g
- Net Carbs: 6g
- Calories: 265

% calories from:
- Fat: 85%
- Carbohydrates: 15%
- Protein: 8%

BACON AND AVOCADO
DEVILED EGGS

GF **DF** **P**

 Difficulty level : 2

 Cost : $$

 15 mins (plus time in fridge)

 15 mins

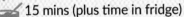 Serves 3

INGREDIENTS:

- 1 ripe avocado
- 4 large eggs, hard-boiled
- 4 slices bacon, cooked and crumbled (use organic nitrate-free bacon for a Paleo version)
- 1 red chili pepper, seeded and minced
- 1 garlic clove, minced
- 2 Tbsp. lemon juice
- Salt and pepper to taste

DIRECTIONS:

1. Peel the eggs, halve them lengthwise and transfer the yolks to a mixing bowl.

2. Add the avocado, chili pepper, garlic and lemon juice to the bowl.

3. Mash with a fork until well combined. Season with salt and pepper to taste.

4. Scoop the mixture into the egg whites and top with the crumbled bacon.

5. Refrigerate until cold or serve right away!

Cooking Tips: Alternatively, use a food processor or hand blender to mash the avocado mixture.

If you want an even creamier filling, add one or two tablespoons of heavy cream to the mixture.

NUTRITION FACTS (PER SERVING)

- Total Carbohydrates: 8g
- Dietary Fiber: 5g
- Protein: 25g
- Total Fat: 37g
- Net Carbs: 3g
- Calories: 455

% calories from:
- Fat: 73%
- Carbohydrates: 7%
- Protein: 22%

BACON AND MOZZARELLA DATES

GF

 Difficulty level : 2

 Cost : $$

 5 mins

 20 mins

 Serves 5

INGREDIENTS:

- 5 medjool dates, pitted and chopped
- 5 slices bacon
- 1 ½ cups mozzarella cheese, sliced

DIRECTIONS:

1. Preheat the oven to 375°F and grease a baking sheet.

2. Heat a large skillet over medium heat. Cook the bacon for about 2 minutes per side, until almost cooked through but still pliable.

3. Wrap some chopped dates in a cheese slice then wrap with half a slice of bacon. Secure with a toothpick and place on the baking sheet. Repeat until all of the ingredients are used.

4. Bake for about 10 minutes, until the bacon is crisp. Serve immediately!

Cooking Tip: Take care not to overcook the bacon so that it's easier to wrap the fillings.

NUTRITION FACTS (PER SERVING)

- Total Carbohydrates: 6g
- Dietary Fiber: 1g
- Protein: 9g
- Total Fat: 9g
- Net Carbs: 5g
- Calories: 142

% calories from:
- Fat: 57%
- Carbohydrates: 17%
- Protein: 25%

CHIPOTLE LIME KALE CHIPS

GF **DF** **P**

 Difficulty level : 1

 Cost : $

 5 mins

 30 mins

 Serves 3

INGREDIENTS:

- 1 large bunch of kale, stems removed
- 2 tsp. lime juice
- 1 tsp. lime zest
- 1 tsp. chipotle powder
- 3 Tbsp. olive oil
- Salt and pepper to taste

DIRECTIONS:

1. Preheat the oven to 325°F. Prepare two baking sheets with parchment paper.

2. In a large bowl, combine the kale leaves with the lime juice, zest and olive oil.

3. Toss until the leaves are well coated.

4. Spread the kale leaves onto the baking sheets in an even layer. Sprinkle with the chipotle powder, pepper and salt.

5. Bake for about 30 minutes or until crisp.

Cooking Tip: Instead of chipotle powder to season the kale, use any spices or herbs of your liking.

NUTRITION FACTS (PER SERVING)

- Total Carbohydrates: 8g
- Dietary Fiber: 2g
- Protein: 2g
- Total Fat: 14g
- Net Carbs: 6g
- Calories: 160

% calories from:
- Fat: 79%
- Carbohydrates: 20%
- Protein: 5%

CARROT FRIES WITH HERB SAUCE (GF)

 Difficulty level : 2

 Cost : $

 5 mins

 25 mins

 Serves 5

INGREDIENTS:

Fries

- 5 carrots
- 1 Tbsp. butter, melted
- 3 Tbsp. olive oil
- Salt and pepper to taste

Herb Sauce

- 5 Tbsp. sour cream
- 5 Tbsp. heavy cream
- 1 Tbsp. fresh thyme, chopped
- 1 tsp. fresh oregano, chopped
- ¼ tsp. fresh rosemary, chopped
- 4 Tbsp. Parmesan cheese, grated
- Salt and pepper to taste

DIRECTIONS:

1. Preheat the oven to 350°F. Prepare a baking sheet with parchment paper or non-stick cooking spray.

2. Cut the carrots into even pieces about the size of French fries.

3. Place in a large mixing bowl and toss with the olive oil, melted butter, salt and pepper. Transfer to the prepared baking sheet and bake for about 30 minutes, flipping halfway through.

4. While the carrots bake, prepare the herb sauce by combining the sour cream with the heavy cream, cheese and fresh herbs. Season with salt and pepper to taste. Mix until smooth.

5. Remove the fries from the oven and serve alongside the herb sauce.

Cooking Tips: No need to peel the carrots, just wash them and cut them into fries with the skin on.

As the herb sauce is better if served cold, prepare it in advance and refrigerate.

NUTRITION FACTS (PER SERVING)

- Total Carbohydrates: 8g
- Dietary Fiber: 2g
- Protein: 4g
- Total Fat: 21g
- Net Carbs: 6g
- Calories: 225

% calories from:
- Fat: 84%
- Carbohydrates: 14%
- Protein: 7%

ZESTY ONION RINGS

GF DF P

 Difficulty level : 2

 Cost : $

 15 mins

 20 mins

 Serves 4

INGREDIENTS:

- 1 large onion, sliced into rings
- ½ cup almond flour
- 1 egg
- ½ tsp. garlic powder
- 1 tsp. paprika
- 1 tsp. cayenne pepper
- 1 tsp. salt

DIRECTIONS:

1. Start by preheating the oven to 400°F and lining a baking sheet with parchment paper.

2. Add the egg to a mixing bowl and then add the almond flour and seasoning to another bowl. Stir the almond flour mixture well.

3. Dip the sliced onions into the egg mixture, followed
   by the almond flour mix, covering both sides of the
   sliced onions.

4. Add the onion rings to the baking sheet and bake for about 10 minutes on each side or until crispy.

NUTRITION FACTS (PER SERVING)	
• Total Carbohydrates: 4g	% calories from:
• Dietary Fiber: 1g	
• Protein: 3g	• Fat:
• Total Fat: 3g	• Carbohydrates:
• Net Carbs: 3g	• Protein:
• Calories: 51	

PIES

ALMOND
BUTTER PIE GF

Difficulty level : 3

Cost : $$$

30 minutes (plus freezing time)

40 minutes

Serves 12

INGREDIENTS:

Crust

- 2 cups whole unroasted almonds
- 1 stick of butter
- 5 Tbsp. coconut flour
- 3 tsp. stevia
- 4 egg whites, beaten
- ¼ tsp. baking soda
- ¼ cup cocoa powder
- ¼ cup whole milk
- Pinch of salt

Filling

- 2 cups whole unroasted almonds
- 2 tbsp. coconut oil, melted
- 3 tsp. stevia
- 1 cup heavy whipping cream, whipped to stiff peaks
- ½ tsp. pure vanilla extract

Topping

- 2 tsp. butter
- ¼ cup sugar-free chocolate chips

. . . .

Cooking Tip: The almond butter can be prepared with raw almonds but toasting them brings more flavors to the recipe.

Serving Suggestions: Use the melted chocolate to create a beautiful decoration and maybe sprinkle some sliced almonds or coconut flakes on top.

DIRECTIONS:

1. Preheat the oven to 350°F and grease a pie pan.

2. To prepare the almond butter for the filling, line a baking sheet with parchment paper and spread the almonds out evenly on it.

3. Bake the almonds until browned, which should take about 10 minutes. Add them to a food processor with the coconut oil until a soft butter is formed, adding more coconut oil if needed.

4. To prepare the crust, combine the butter and almonds in food processor, mix until creamy.

5. Transfer the mixture to a bowl. Add the coconut flour, cocoa powder, baking soda, salt, stevia and egg whites to the bowl, and mix well.

6. Add the milk one tablespoon at a time, until a dough is formed. It should be slightly soft.

7. Press into the bottom and sides of the pie pan. Bake for about 15 minutes, until browned. Allow to cool and transfer to the refrigerator.

8. With a hand mixer, beat the prepared almond butter, vanilla and stevia until smooth and creamy.

9. Gently fold in the whipped cream and mix until just combined. Pour into the cooled crust and freeze for at least 2 hours.

10. Just before serving, melt the chocolate chips with the butter and mix well. Drizzle over the pie and serve.

NUTRITION FACTS (PER SERVING)

- Total Carbohydrates: 16g
- Dietary Fiber: 8g
- Protein: 13g
- Total Fat: 45g
- Net Carbs: 8g
- Calories: 496

% calories from:
- Fat: 82%
- Carbohydrates: 13%
- Protein: 10%

PUMPKIN PIE (GF)

Difficulty level : 3
Cost : $$
20 mins
60 mins
Serves 3

INGREDIENTS:

Crust

- 4 Tbsp. coconut flour
- 1 cup almond flour
- ½ cup coconut flakes
- ½ cup heavy cream
- 5 Tbsp. whole milk
- 1 tsp. stevia

Filling

- ½ cup heavy cream
- ½ cup coconut milk
- 1 ½ cups pure pumpkin puree
- 1 tsp. stevia
- 4 eggs
- 1 tsp. cinnamon
- ½ tsp. nutmeg
- ¼ tsp. clove
- Pinch of salt

Topping

- 1 cup heavy whipping cream
- 1 tsp. stevia

DIRECTIONS:

1. Preheat the oven to 350°F and grease a pie pan.

2. To prepare the crust, mix the almond flour, coconut flour, coconut flakes, stevia and heavy cream together in a medium bowl, until well combined. Add the whole milk one tablespoon at a time, until a soft dough is formed. Press the mixture into the pie pan and bake for about 10 minutes. Remove from the oven and allow to cool.

3. In a large bowl, mix together all of the filling ingredients with an electric mixer until smooth and creamy. Pour into the prepared crust and bake at 325°F for 50 minutes, until the center is set. Cool on a wire rack.

4. To prepare the topping, whip the heavy cream with the stevia until stiff peaks form.

5. Serve each slice with a generous dollop of the topping and enjoy!

Cooking Tip: You may need to add more coconut flour or heavy cream to the crust mixture to adjust the texture. It should be soft and easy to press into the pie pan.

NUTRITION FACTS (PER SERVING)

- Total Carbohydrates: 11g
- Dietary Fiber: 4g
- Protein: 7g
- Total Fat: 30g
- Net Carbs: 7g
- Calories: 326

% calories from:
- Fat: 83%
- Carbohydrates: 13%
- Protein: 9%

COCONUT CREAM PIE GF

 Difficulty level : 2

 Cost : $$

 20 minutes (plus time in fridge)

 30 mins

 Serves 8

INGREDIENTS:

Crust

- 1 cup toasted almonds, finely chopped
- ½ cup unsweetened coconut flakes
- 4 Tbsp. coconut flour
- ½ cup butter (use coconut oil for a Paleo version)
- 2 tsp. raw stevia

Filling

- 1 ½ cups unsweetened coconut flakes
- 1 ½ cups full fat unsweetened coconut milk
- 3 eggs
- 2 tsp. raw stevia
- 1 tsp. pure vanilla extract
- ¼ cup unsweetened coconut flakes, toasted

Cooking Tip: Place the pie in the freezer for about 1 hour, instead of refrigerating it, if you are short on time.

DIRECTIONS:

1. Preheat the oven to 325°F and prepare a pie pan with non-stick cooking spray.

2. To prepare the crust, mix the almonds, coconut flakes, coconut flour and stevia together in a small bowl. Stir in the butter using a fork and mix until well combined. Add a little water if needed.

3. Press the mixture into the prepared pie pan and bake for about 15 minutes. Remove from the oven and allow to cool.

4. To prepare the filling, combine the coconut milk, stevia and vanilla extract in a saucepan over medium heat. Bring to a simmer.

5. In a small bowl, whisk the egg together with a bit of the hot coconut milk (this tempers the egg to keep it from scrambling in the hot liquid). Add to the saucepan, reduce the heat to low and allow to cook for about 5 minutes, until slightly thickened.

6. Remove from the heat and allow to cool to room temperature. Stir in the unsweetened coconut flakes and pour into the prepared crust. Cover with plastic wrap and refrigerate for at least 2 hours.

7. Top the pie with toasted coconut flakes and serve!

NUTRITION FACTS (PER SERVING)

- Total Carbohydrates: 13g
- Dietary Fiber: 7g
- Protein: 8g
- Total Fat: 41g
- Net Carbs: 6g
- Calories: 428

% calories from:
- Fat: 86%
- Carbohydrates: 12%
- Protein: 7%

DARK CHOCOLATE TART

GF

 Difficulty level : 2

 Cost : $$

 20 minutes (plus time in fridge)

 30 minutes

Serves 10

INGREDIENTS:

Crust

- 1 cup coconut flour
- ¼ cup flaxseed meal
- 1 Tbsp. erythritol
- ½ cup butter
- 4 egg whites

Filling

- ½ cup cocoa powder
- 1 cup heavy cream
- 2 ½ tsp. gelatin powder
- 2 tsp. stevia
- 1 tsp. pure vanilla extract
- ¼ cup pistachios, sliced

DIRECTIONS:

1. Preheat the oven to 375°F and prepare a small tart or pie pan with non-stick cooking spray.

2. In a food processor, combine all of the crust ingredients and pulse until well combined. Press the mixture into the prepared tart pan and bake for about 15 minutes. Remove from the oven and allow to cool.

3. To prepare the filling, combine all of the filling ingredients, except the pistachios, in a blender or food processor and blend until smooth and creamy.

4. Pour the mixture into the crust, cover with plastic wrap, and refrigerate for at least 2 hours.

5. Sprinkle with the pistachios and serve.

Cooking Tip: The time required in the refrigerator may vary so keep an eye on the texture of the filling - it must be firm at the center.

NUTRITION FACTS (PER SERVING)

- Total Carbohydrates: 14g
- Dietary Fiber: 7g
- Protein: 6g
- Total Fat: 23g
- Net Carbs: 7g
- Calories: 268

% calories from:
- Fat: 77%
- Carbohydrates: 21%
- Protein: 9%

LEMON BLUEBERRY CHEESECAKE

GF

👤 Difficulty level : 2

💲 Cost : $$

🥣 20 minutes (plus time in fridge)

🕐 30 minutes

🔔 Serves 8

INGREDIENTS:

Crust

- 1 cup unsweetened coconut flakes
- 1 cup butter
- 1 cup almond flour
- 1 pinch salt

Filling

- 1 cup blueberries (fresh or frozen)
- 1 lemon, juiced
- 2 tsp. lemon zest
- 2 (8-ounce) packages cream cheese, softened
- ¼ cup heavy cream
- 1 Tbsp. gelatin
- 2 tsp. stevia
- 1 tsp. fresh mint leaves, chopped

. . . .

Cooking Tip: You can add strawberries and raspberries to this pie, but remember to bear your macros in mind!

DIRECTIONS:

1. Preheat the oven to 375°F and grease a medium pie pan.

2. To prepare the crust, pulse all of the crust ingredients together in a food processor until well combined. Add more almond flour or butter if needed, the texture should be soft. Press the crust into the pie pan.

3. Bake the crust in the preheated oven for 15 minutes or until browned. Let it cool.

4. For the filling, add the blueberries and lemon juice to a small saucepan over medium heat. Bring to a simmer and cook for about 10 minutes. Remove from the heat, add lemon zest and allow to cool slightly.

5. In a blender or food processor, combine the cream cheese, heavy cream, gelatin, fresh mint and stevia. Blend until smooth and creamy.

6. Pour the cream cheese mixture into the prepared crust.

7. Spoon the blueberries on top of the cream cheese mixture and gently swirl with a sharp knife or skewer.

8. Cover with plastic wrap and refrigerate for several hours or overnight.

9. Slice, serve and enjoy.

NUTRITION FACTS (PER SERVING)

- Total Carbohydrates: 12g
- Dietary Fiber: 3g
- Protein: 7g
- Total Fat: 56g
- Net Carbs: 9g
- Calories: 556

% calories from:
- Fat: 91%
- Carbohydrates: 9%
- Protein: 5%

DESSERTS

EASY CHOCOLATE MUG GF CAKE

 Difficulty level : 1

 Cost : $

 5 mins

 3 mins

 Serves 2

INGREDIENTS:

- 1 Tbsp. coconut flour
- ¼ cup almond flour
- 2 tsp. raw stevia
- 3 Tbsp. raw unsweetened cocoa powder
- 2 eggs, beaten
- 3 Tbsp. heavy cream (use full fat unsweetened coconut milk for a Paleo version)
- ¼ tsp. cinnamon
- ½ tsp. gluten free baking powder (use baking soda for a Paleo version)
- Pinch of nutmeg
- Pinch of salt

DIRECTIONS:

1. In a small bowl, whisk together all of the ingredients until no lumps remain. The mixture should be slightly thick, so add more heavy cream or almond flour as needed.

2. Divide evenly between two microwave-safe mugs.

3. Microwave one mug on high for 60 seconds.

4. The cake should be springy to the touch and slightly puffed. If additional cooking time is needed, microwave on high in 15 second intervals.

5. Repeat with the second mug. Cooking them separately ensures even cooking.

Cooking Tip: Adjust the amount of cocoa powder according to your preference.

NUTRITION FACTS (PER SERVING)

- Total Carbohydrates: 14g
- Dietary Fiber: 6g
- Protein: 11g
- Total Fat: 21g
- Net Carbs: 8g
- Calories: 257

% calories from:
- Fat: 74%
- Carbohydrates: 22%
- Protein: 17%

HAZELNUT BROWNIES GF

 Difficulty level : 2

 Cost : $$

 15 mins

 30 mins

 Serves 5

INGREDIENTS:

- ½ cup cocoa powder
- ¾ cup almond flour
- 1 Tbsp. flax meal
- 8 eggs
- 1 Tbsp. erythritol
- ½ cup hazelnuts, toasted and coarsely chopped
- ½ cup butter, melted
- 1 tsp. pure vanilla extract
- Pinch of salt

DIRECTIONS:

1. Preheat the oven to 350°F. Prepare a baking dish with non-stick cooking spray.

2. In a large bowl, whisk together the cocoa powder, almond flour, flax meal, erythritol and salt until well combined.

3. In a separate bowl, whisk the eggs together with the vanilla extract and melted butter.

4. Stir the eggs into the dry ingredients and mix until smooth. Stir in the chopped hazelnuts.

5. Transfer to the prepared baking dish and bake for 25 minutes, or until a toothpick inserted comes out clean.

6. Cool on a wire rack, slice and serve.

. . . .

Serving Suggestion: Try serving with keto ice cream.

NUTRITION FACTS (PER SERVING)

- Total Carbohydrates: 14g
- Dietary Fiber: 6g
- Protein: 16g
- Total Fat: 42g
- Net Carbs: 8g
- Calories: 463

% calories from:
- Fat: 82%
- Carbohydrates: 12%
- Protein: 14%

NEW YORK STYLE CHEESECAKE

GF

 Difficulty level : 2

 Cost : $

15 minutes (plus time in fridge)

 30 minutes

Serves 5

INGREDIENTS:

- 2 (8-ounce) packages cream cheese
- 4 large eggs
- 2 Tbsp. erythritol
- ¼ cup sour cream
- 1 tsp. pure vanilla extract
- ¼ cup berries for garnish

DIRECTIONS:

1. Preheat the oven to 325°F. Prepare two small pie pans with non-stick cooking spray.

2. In a large bowl, beat the cream cheese and erythritol together with a hand mixer until light and fluffy.

3. Add the eggs one at a time and continue mixing until smooth.

4. Stir in the sour cream and vanilla extract.

5. Pour the mixture into the pie pans and bake for about 30 minutes, until the centers of the cheesecakes are set and the edges are lightly browned.

6. Transfer to a wire rack and allow to cool to room temperature. Then, refrigerate for several hours or overnight.

7. Serve alongside fresh fruit. Blueberries, raspberries and strawberries are a great combination

Cooking Tip: Use pie pans of any size to prepare the cheesecakes. Just remember to adjust the baking time accordingly – they are ready when the center is set.

Serving Suggestion: Try serving with keto strawberry sauce on top.

NUTRITION FACTS (PER SERVING)

- Total Carbohydrates: 10g
- Dietary Fiber: 0g
- Protein: 10g
- Total Fat: 37g
- Net Carbs: 10g
- Calories: 388

% calories from:
- Fat: 86%
- Carbohydrates: 10%
- Protein: 10%

CLASSIC CARROT CAKE

GF

Difficulty level : 2

Cost : $$

15 minutes

30 minutes

Serves 12

INGREDIENTS:

- Batter
- 1 cup carrots, finely grated
- 2 Tbsp. erythritol
- 1 cup butter, softened
- 2 cups almond flour
- ¼ cup coconut flour
- 5 eggs
- 1 ½ cups water
- ½ tsp. baking soda
- 1 tsp. gluten free baking powder
- 1 tsp. cinnamon
- ½ tsp. clove powder
- ½ tsp. nutmeg
- Cream Cheese Frosting
- 1 cup cream cheese, softened
- 1 tsp. pure vanilla extract
- ¼ cup toasted walnuts, chopped

DIRECTIONS:

1. Preheat the oven to 350°F. Grease a round cake pan with butter or oil.

2. To start preparing the batter, use a hand mixer to blend together the erythritol, butter and eggs.

3. In a separate bowl, whisk together the dry ingredients until well combined.

4. Slowly add the dry ingredients to the wet ingredients and keep blending until no lumps remain.

5. Stir in the grated carrots and then gradually add the water until a thick batter is formed. Pour into the prepared cake pan and bake for about 30 minutes, or until a toothpick inserted comes out clean.

6. Remove from the oven and allow to cool.

7. To prepare the frosting, beat the cream cheese and vanilla extract until light and fluffy.

8. Top the cake with the frosting and toasted walnuts, slice and serve.

NUTRITION FACTS (PER SERVING)

• Total Carbohydrates: 10g	% calories from:
• Dietary Fiber: 3g	• Fat: 86%
• Protein: 8g	• Carbohydrates: 11%
• Total Fat: 35g	• Protein: 9%
• Net Carbs: 7g	
• Calories: 365	

Cooking Tips: You can replace the orange juice in the frosting with lemon juice. Lemon or orange zests also add more flavor and texture.

ALMOND FLOUR GF
SNICKERDOOLES

 Difficulty level : 2

 Cost : $

 10 minutes (plus time in fridge)

15 minutes

 Serves 6

INGREDIENTS:

- 6 Tbsp. butter, softened
- 2 eggs, beaten
- 1 cup almond flour
- 2 Tbsp. heavy cream
- 4 tsp. stevia
- ½ tsp. pure vanilla extract
- ½ tsp. gluten free baking powder
- 1 ½ tsp. cinnamon
- 1 pinch nutmeg
- 1 pinch salt

DIRECTIONS:

1. Preheat the oven to 350°F and prepare a baking sheet with parchment paper or non-stick cooking spray.

2. In a large bowl, combine the almond flour, gluten free baking powder, 2 teaspoons of stevia, nutmeg and salt.

3. Stir in the butter, heavy cream, eggs and vanilla extract, and mix until well combined. Cover with plastic wrap and refrigerate for about 30 minutes.

4. In a small, shallow dish, mix together the cinnamon and the remaining stevia.

5. Divide the cookie dough into six even portions and roll each one between your hands to form a ball. Drop each ball into the cinnamon/stevia mixture and toss to coat.

6. Place on the baking sheet and flatten with a heavy glass or jar with a flat base.

7. Bake for about 15 minutes, or until the edges are golden brown.

8. Transfer to a wire rack and allow to cool. Enjoy!

Cooking Tip: The dough should be firm but easy to roll, so add more almond flour if needed.

NUTRITION FACTS (PER SERVING)

- Total Carbohydrates: 7g
- Dietary Fiber: 2g
- Protein: 6g
- Total Fat: 24g
- Net Carbs: 5g
- Calories: 251

% calories from:
- Fat: 86%
- Carbohydrates: 11%
- Protein: 10%

CREAMY COCONUT
DOUBLE CHOCOLATE

HOT COCOA

GF

 Difficulty level : 1

 Cost : $

 5 mins

 10 mins

🔔 Serves 3

INGREDIENTS:

- 1 cup full-fat unsweetened coconut milk
- 1 Tbsp. raw unsweetened cocoa powder
- 1 Tbsp. erythritol
- 1 tsp. pure vanilla extract
- 1 Tbsp. dark chocolate chips
- 2 Tbsp. whipped cream for topping (optional)

DIRECTIONS:

1. Start by adding the coconut milk to the base of a stockpot over a low/medium heat. Add the cocoa powder and whisk to combine.

2. Add in the erythritol and vanilla extract and whisk for about 5 minutes until warmed through.

3. Pour the hot cocoa into 3 mugs and top with the whipped cream and chocolate chips.

. . . .

Cooking Tip: Add a quarter of a teaspoon of pure peppermint extract to make a peppermint hot cocoa, if desired.

NUTRITION FACTS (PER SERVING)

- Total Carbohydrates: 13g
- Dietary Fiber: 2g
- Protein: 3g
- Total Fat: 23g
- Net Carbs: 11g
- Calories: 233

% calories from:
- Fat: 79%
- Carbohydrates: 11%
- Protein: 5%

COCONUT BROWNIE SUNDAE

GF **DF**

Difficulty level : 2

Cost : $

15 mins

40-45 mins

Serves 8

INGREDIENTS:

- 2 Tbsp. coconut flour, sifted
- 3 Tbsp. raw unsweetened cocoa powder
- ½ cup coconut oil, melted
- 2 eggs
- 1 tsp. pure vanilla extract
- ¼ cup erythritol
- 2 cups full-fat unsweetened coconut milk (canned)

DIRECTIONS:

1. Start by preheating the oven to 325°F and greasing a baking dish with coconut oil.

2. Add all of the ingredients, minus the coconut milk, to a food processor and blend until smooth.

3. Pour the batter into the greased baking dish and bake for 40-45 minutes or until a knife inserted into the center comes out clean.

4. While the brownies are cooking, add the solid part from the can of coconut milk to a food processor and process until a whipped cream consistency forms.

5. Pour the whipped coconut milk into a bowl and chill it in the fridge until the brownies are cooked.

6. Serve the brownies with the whipped coconut cream.

NUTRITION FACTS (PER SERVING)

	% calories from:
- Total Carbohydrates: 12g	
- Dietary Fiber: 2g	- Fat: 83%
- Protein: 3g	- Carbohydrates: 13%
- Total Fat: 28g	- Protein: 4%
- Net Carbs: 10g	
- Calories: 266	

Cooking Tip: Add 1 tablespoon of raw unsweetened cocoa powder to the coconut milk for a double chocolate "sundae" and/or a teaspoon of pure vanilla extract.

MEAT DISHES

BUFFALO CHICKEN WINGS

 Difficulty level : 1

 Cost : $

 10 mins

 45 mins

Serves 4

INGREDIENTS:

- 12 chicken wings
- ¼ cup no-sugar-added hot sauce (gluten free)
- ¼ cup butter, melted
- ¼ tsp. salt

DIRECTIONS:

1. Start by preheating the oven to 425°F and greasing a baking dish with coconut oil.

2. Add the chicken wings with the hot sauce, melted butter and salt to a large mixing bowl and toss to cover the wings in the sauce.

3. Add the wings to the baking dish and bake for about 45 minutes or until the wings are cooked through.

. . . .

Cooking Tip: Serve with blue cheese, if desired.

NUTRITION FACTS (PER SERVING)

- Total Carbohydrates: 10g
- Dietary Fiber: 0g
- Protein: 18g
- Total Fat: 31g
- Net Carbs: 10g
- Calories: 385

% calories from:
- Fat: 71%
- Carbohydrates: 10%
- Protein: 18%

BALSAMIC MEATLOAF
GF **DF**

 Difficulty level : 2

 Cost : $$

 10 mins

 60 mins

 Serves 6

INGREDIENTS:

- 1 lb. ground beef
- 1 yellow onion, finely chopped
- 2 cloves garlic, chopped
- 2 Tbsp. tomato paste
- ¼ cup balsamic vinegar (gluten free)
- 1 Tbsp. Italian seasoning
- 1 tsp. salt
- ½ tsp. black pepper
- Coconut oil for greasing

DIRECTIONS:

1. Start by preheating the oven to 350°F and greasing a 9 x 5 loaf pan with coconut oil.

2. Add all of the ingredients to a large mixing bowl and mix well.

3. Add the mixture to the greased loaf pan and bake
for 55-60 minutes or until the meatloaf is cooked all the way through.

4. Cool for 10 minutes before slicing.

Cooking Tip: Serve with a drizzle of ketchup, if desired, keeping in mind that this will raise the carbohydrate count. Skip the ketchup for a lower carb version.

NUTRITION FACTS (PER SERVING)

- Total Carbohydrates: 4g
- Dietary Fiber: 1g
- Protein: 24g
- Total Fat: 6g
- Net Carbs: 3g
- Calories: 163

% calories from:
- Fat: 33%
- Carbohydrates: 7%
- Protein: 59%

HERB "FRIED" CHICKEN

GF DF P

 Difficulty level : 2

 Cost : $

 15 mins

 20-25 mins

 Serves 4

INGREDIENTS:

- 4 boneless skinless chicken breasts
- 1 egg
- ½ cup almond flour
- ½ tsp. onion powder
- 1 tsp. garlic powder
- 1 Tbsp. Italian seasoning
- ½ tsp. paprika
- 1 tsp. salt
- Coconut oil for greasing

DIRECTIONS:

1. Start by preheating the oven to 350°F and greasing a baking dish with coconut oil.

2. Add the egg to a small bowl and then add the almond flour with the seasoning to another bowl.

3. Dip the chicken breasts into the egg mixture, covering both sides, and then dip into the almond flour mixture, again covering both sides.

4. Add the chicken breasts to the baking dish and bake for 20-25 minutes or until the chicken is no longer pink in the middle. Flip the chicken halfway through.

. . . .

Cooking Tip: Try experimenting with different herbs and add a combination that you like best.

NUTRITION FACTS (PER SERVING)

• Total Carbohydrates: 2g	% calories from:
• Dietary Fiber: 1g	• Fat: 42%
• Protein: 45g	• Carbohydrates: 1%
• Total Fat: 15g	• Protein: 45%
• Net Carbs: 1g	
• Calories: 328	

SOUPS & SAUCES

BOLOGNESE SAUCE

GF

 Difficulty level : 2

 Cost : $

 10 mins

 10-15 mins

 Serves 4

INGREDIENTS:

- 1 lb. ground beef
- 1 (28 ounce) can diced tomatoes
- 2 cloves garlic, chopped
- 1 tsp. thyme, freshly chopped
- ½ tsp. rosemary, freshly chopped
- 1 Tbsp. basil, freshly chopped
- 1 tsp. salt
- 2 Tbsp. butter

DIRECTIONS:

1. Start by heating a large stockpot over a medium heat with the butter.
2. Add the ground beef and cook until brown.
3. Add the remaining ingredients and cook for 5-10 minutes until warmed through.
4. Serve with zucchini noodles or spaghetti squash.

NUTRITION FACTS (PER SERVING)

- Total Carbohydrates: 9g
- Dietary Fiber: 3g
- Protein: 36g
- Total Fat: 13g
- Net Carbs: 6g
- Calories: 301

% calories from:
- Fat: 41%
- Carbohydrates: 8%
- Protein: 51%

QUICK & SIMPLE
FRENCH ONION
SOUP GF

 Difficulty level : 1

 Cost : $

 15 mins

 35 mins

Serves 4

INGREDIENTS:

- 6 cups beef broth
- ½ cup butter
- 2 yellow onions, sliced
- 1 tsp. thyme, freshly chopped
- 1 bay leaf
- 4 slices provolone cheese
- ¼ cup Parmesan cheese, grated
- ½ tsp. salt

DIRECTIONS:

1. Start by preheating a large stockpot over a medium heat with the butter.

2. Add the onions and cook for 4-5 minutes or until soft and browned.

3. Add the remaining ingredients, minus the parmesan cheese and provolone cheese, and stir.

4. Bring the soup to a boil and then simmer for 30 minutes.

5. Remove the bay leaf and top with the two cheeses.

6. Enjoy right away.

NUTRITION FACTS (PER SERVING)

• Total Carbohydrates: 7g	% calories from:
• Dietary Fiber: 1g	• Fat: 77%
• Protein: 17g	• Carbohydrates: 6%
• Total Fat: 34g	• Protein: 17%
• Net Carbs: 6g	
• Calories: 407	

CHEESY ALFREDO
SAUCE GF

 Difficulty level : 1

 Cost : $

 10 mins

 5-7 mins

 Serves 4

INGREDIENTS:

- ½ cup butter
- ¾ cup heavy cream
- 2 cups Parmesan cheese, grated
- 2 cloves garlic, chopped
- 1 tsp. onion powder
- ½ tsp. salt

DIRECTIONS:

1. Start by adding the butter to a saucepan over a low heat and wait until the butter has melted.

2. Add in the remaining ingredients and whisk to combine. Heat for about 5 minutes, until everything is melted and mixed well.

3. Serve over sautéed vegetables or zucchini noodles.

NUTRITION FACTS (PER SERVING)

• Total Carbohydrates: 2g	% calories from:
• Dietary Fiber: 0g	• Fat: 89%
• Protein: 8g	• Carbohydrates: 2%
• Total Fat: 37g	• Protein: 9%
• Net Carbs: 2g	
• Calories: 383	

SLOW COOKER RECIPES

NO BEAN CHILI

 Difficulty level : 2

 Cost : $

 10 mins

 4 hrs

 Serves 6

INGREDIENTS:

- 1 lb. ground turkey
- 1 (28 ounce) can diced tomatoes
- 2 cups chicken broth
- 1 red bell pepper, chopped
- 1 yellow onion, chopped
- 2 cloves garlic, chopped
- 1 cup kale, chopped
- 1 Tbsp. Italian seasoning
- 1 tsp. crushed red pepper flakes
- Salt and pepper to taste
- Coconut oil for cooking
- 1 cup cheddar cheese, shredded, for serving
- 6 Tbsp. sour cream, for serving

DIRECTIONS:

1. Start by adding the coconut oil to the base of a slow cooker along with the ground turkey, bell pepper, kale, seasoning, onion, garlic and red pepper flakes.
2. Cover with the broth and diced tomatoes.
3. Cook on high for 4 hours stirring every hour.
4. Season with salt and pepper and top with the shredded cheese and sour cream.

Cooking Tip: You can use ground beef instead of turkey, if desired.

NUTRITION FACTS (PER SERVING)

- Total Carbohydrates: 6g
- Dietary Fiber: 1g
- Protein: 28g
- Total Fat: 18g
- Net Carbs: 5g
- Calories: 318

% calories from:
- Fat: 55%
- Carbohydrates: 7%
- Protein: 38%

SLOW COOKER
SAUSAGE & PEPPERS

 Difficulty level : 1

 Cost : $

 10 mins

 6 hrs

 Serves 6

DIRECTIONS:

1. Start by adding the sausage, pepper, garlic and onion to the base of a slow cooker.

2. Cover with the diced tomatoes, broth and seasoning.

3. Cook on low for 6 hours.

4. Season with salt and pepper and enjoy.

Cooking Tip: Add crushed red pepper flakes for added heat.

INGREDIENTS:

- 4 Italian sausage links
- 2 green peppers, sliced
- 1 white onion, sliced
- 2 cloves garlic, chopped
- 1 (28 ounce) can diced tomatoes
- ½ cup beef broth
- 1 Tbsp. Italian seasoning
- Salt and pepper to taste

NUTRITION FACTS (PER SERVING)

• Total Carbohydrates: 9g	% calories from:
• Dietary Fiber: 3g	
• Protein: 4g	• Fat: 47%
• Total Fat: 4g	• Carbohydrates: 32%
• Net Carbs: 6g	• Protein: 21%
• Calories: 80	

SLOW COOKER PULLED PORK

 Difficulty level : 1

 Cost : $

 10 mins

 10 mins

 Serves 8

INGREDIENTS:

- 2 lb. pork tenderloin
- 1 yellow onion, chopped
- 2 cloves of garlic, chopped
- 1 cup beef broth
- ¼ cup raw apple cider vinegar
- 1 tsp. garlic powder
- ¼ tsp. cayenne pepper
- Salt & pepper to taste

DIRECTIONS:

1. Start by adding the pork, onion and garlic to the base of a slow cooker.

2. Cover with the broth, apple cider vinegar and seasoning.

3. Cook on low for 10 hours or until the pork is easily pulled apart.

. . . .

Cooking Tip: Add a drizzle of hot sauce for serving, if desired.

NUTRITION FACTS (PER SERVING)

• Total Carbohydrates: 2g	% calories from:
• Dietary Fiber: 0g	
• Protein: 31g	• Fat: 21%
• Total Fat: 4g	• Carbohydrates: 5%
• Net Carbs: 2g	• Protein: 74%
• Calories: 177	

CAULIFLOWER MAC & CHEESE

 Difficulty level : 1

 Cost : $

 10 mins

 4 hrs

 Serves 6

DIRECTIONS:

1. Start by adding the cauliflower to the base of a slow cooker and top with the remaining ingredients.

2. Cook on low for 4 hours and enjoy right away.

Cooking Tip: You can replace the cheddar cheese with monetary jack or mozzarella cheese, if desired.

INGREDIENTS:

- 1 head cauliflower cut into florets
- 2 cups cheddar cheese, shredded
- 1 cup heavy cream
- 1 yellow onion, chopped
- ½ tsp. paprika
- 1 tsp. garlic powder
- ¼ tsp. salt
- 1 pinch black pepper

NUTRITION FACTS (PER SERVING)

• Total Carbohydrates: 6g	% calories from:
• Dietary Fiber: 2g	
• Protein: 11g	• Fat: 75%
• Total Fat: 20g	• Carbohydrates: 7%
• Net Carbs: 4g	• Protein: 18%
• Calories: 241	

BEEF STROGANOFF

Difficulty level : 1

Cost : $

10 mins

6 hrs

Serves 6

INGREDIENTS:

- 1 ½ lbs. beef sirloin steak cut into strips
- 1 yellow onion, chopped
- 2 cloves garlic, chopped
- ½ cup butter
- ½ cup beef broth
- 1 cup cream cheese
- 1 cup cremini mushrooms
- ¼ tsp. salt
- ¼ tsp. black pepper

DIRECTIONS:

1. Start by adding the steak to the base of a slow cooker with the chopped onion, garlic and mushrooms.
2. Add the broth, cream cheese, butter, salt and pepper.
3. Gently stir to combine and cook on low for 6 hours or until the beef is tender.

Cooking Tip: For a creamier flavor, add ½ cup of sour cream.

NUTRITION FACTS (PER SERVING)

- Total Carbohydrates: 4g
- Dietary Fiber: 1g
- Protein: 38g
- Total Fat: 36g
- Net Carbs: 3g
- Calories: 497

% calories from:
- Fat: 66%
- Carbohydrates: 2%
- Protein: 31%

CREAMY BUTTERNUT SQUASH SOUP

 Difficulty level : 1

 Cost : $

 10 mins

 4 hrs

 Serves 6

DIRECTIONS:

1. Start by adding the butternut squash, carrots, onion and garlic to the base of a slow cooker.

2. Add in all the remaining ingredients, minus the cheddar cheese, and cook on low for 4 hours.

3. Serve with the shredded cheddar cheese.

Cooking Tip: You can replace the cubed butternut squash for cubed sweet potato, if desired.

INGREDIENTS:

- 3 cups of butternut squash, cubed
- 1 yellow onion, chopped
- 2 cloves garlic, chopped
- 2 carrots, chopped
- ½ cup butter
- 1 cup heavy cream
- ¼ tsp. dried rosemary
- ¼ tsp. dried sage
- ½ tsp. salt
- ¼ tsp. black pepper
- 1 cup cheddar cheese, shredded, for serving

NUTRITION FACTS (PER SERVING)

- Total Carbohydrates: 13g
- Dietary Fiber: 2g
- Protein: 6g
- Total Fat: 29g
- Net Carbs: 11g
- Calories: 330

% calories from:
- Fat: 79%
- Carbohydrates: 13%
- Protein: 7%

CREAMY RANCH
CHICKEN

 Difficulty level : 1

 Cost : $

 10 mins

 4 hrs

 Serves 4

INGREDIENTS:

- 4 boneless skinless chicken breasts
- 1 yellow onion, chopped
- 1 clove garlic, chopped
- 1 green bell pepper, seeded and chopped
- 1 (28 ounce) can diced tomatoes
- 1 cup heavy cream
- 1 cup whole milk
- 1 cup cheddar cheese, shredded
- ¼ tsp. paprika
- ½ tsp. salt

DIRECTIONS:

1. Start by adding the chicken to the base of a slow cooker with the onion, garlic, pepper and diced tomatoes.

2. Add in the heavy cream, whole milk, seasoning and cheddar cheese.

3. Cook on low for 4 hours.

. . . .

Cooking Tip: You can replace the chicken breasts with turkey, if desired.

NUTRITION FACTS (PER SERVING)

- Total Carbohydrates: 17g
- Dietary Fiber: 3g
- Protein: 34g
- Total Fat: 26g
- Net Carbs: 14g
- Calories: 432

% calories from:
- Fat: 55%
- Carbohydrates: 13%
- Protein: 32%

CLASSIC
CHICKEN SOUP

 Difficulty level : 1

 Cost : $

 10 mins

 4-6 hrs

 Serves 4

INGREDIENTS:

- 4 boneless skinless chicken breasts
- 1 yellow onion, chopped
- 1 clove garlic, chopped
- 2 carrots, chopped
- 2 stalks celery, chopped
- 6 cups chicken broth
- ¼ cup parsley, freshly chopped
- 1 tsp. salt
- ¼ tsp. pepper

DIRECTIONS:

1. Start by adding the chicken to the base of a slow cooker.

2. Add in the remaining ingredients and cook on low for 4-6 hours.

3. Shred the chicken using two forks before serving.

. . . .

Cooking Tip: You can replace the chicken breasts with turkey, if desired.

NUTRITION FACTS (PER SERVING)

- Total Carbohydrates: 8g
- Dietary Fiber: 2g
- Protein: 29g
- Total Fat: 5g
- Net Carbs: 6g
- Calories: 199

% calories from:
- Fat: 24%
- Carbohydrates: 13%
- Protein: 63%

BALSAMIC
BEEF STEW

 Difficulty level : 1

 Cost : $

 10 mins

 6 hrs

 Serves 4

INGREDIENTS:

- 1 lb. sirloin steak, cubed
- 1 red onion, sliced
- 3 cloves garlic, chopped
- 2 carrots, chopped
- ¼ cup balsamic vinegar
- 1 cup beef broth
- ¼ cup parsley, freshly chopped
- 1 tsp. salt
- ¼ tsp. pepper
- ¼ cup sour cream for serving

DIRECTIONS:

1. Start by adding the sirloin steak to the base of a slow cooker.

2. Add in the remaining ingredients and cook on low for 6 hours.

3. Serve with a dollop of sour cream per serving.

· ·

Cooking Tip: You can replace the chicken breasts with turkey, if desired.

NUTRITION FACTS (PER SERVING)

- Total Carbohydrates: 8g
- Dietary Fiber: 2g
- Protein: 37g
- Total Fat: 11g
- Net Carbs: 6g
- Calories: 283

% calories from:
- Fat: 37%
- Carbohydrates: 9%
- Protein: 55%

CREAMY MUSHROOM CHICKEN

 Difficulty level : 1

 Cost : $

 10 mins

 4 hrs

 Serves 6

INGREDIENTS:

- 6 boneless skinless chicken breasts
- 1 yellow onion, chopped
- 1 cup heavy cream
- 1 cup cream cheese
- 1 cup cremini mushrooms
- ¼ tsp. paprika
- 1 tsp. salt
- ¼ tsp. pepper

DIRECTIONS:

1. Start by adding the chicken breasts, mushrooms and onion to the base of a slow cooker.

2. Add in the remaining ingredients and cook on low for 4 hours.

Cooking Tip: Serve with shredded cheese, if desired.

NUTRITION FACTS (PER SERVING)

- Total Carbohydrates: 4g
- Dietary Fiber: 1g
- Protein: 25g
- Total Fat: 23g
- Net Carbs: 3g
- Calories: 329

% calories from:
- Fat: 65%
- Carbohydrates: 4%
- Protein: 31%